Spiritual Mind Power Affirmations

Practical, Mystical, and Spiritual Inspiration Applied to Your Life

Spiritual Mind Power Affirmations
Practical, Mystical, and Spiritual Inspiration Applied to Your Life
University of Sedona Publishing
2675 W. State Route 89A, Suite 465
Sedona, Arizona 86336
www.universityofsedona.com

Library of Congress Control Number: 2017940045
Masters, Paul Leon.
Spiritual Mind Power Affirmations
/ Paul Leon Masters. – 1st ed.
ISBN 978-0-9964596-1-7
1. Meditation. 2. Mind and Body. 3. Metaphysics.

Disclaimer

The content of this book is not intended to replace any form of professionally licensed care, be it medical, psychological, or any other licensed health modality. The views and ideas expressed, whether in totality or as an adjunct to one's spiritual or religious beliefs, are for use in one's spiritual life. Nothing in the content of this book should be considered as infallible, as life is an ongoing process of awakening to truths and practices known only to God.

PRINTED IN THE UNITED STATES OF AMERICA

PRAISE FOR DR. MASTERS

Dr. Master's has given me so much. Before I came to the University of Metaphysics, I never saw the value in affirmations. Today, I can attest that without the use of affirmations I would not be seeing the Divine in all of God's creation.

Let me relate a short story of something that recently happened to me. I was taking a walk outside my office. As I looked around me, I was awestruck by the beauty of everything. Every cloud, every tree seemed to be filled with God. It was like a subtle glow. An illumination from within. It wasn't so much a visual experience, as a spiritual one. I knew then that all the trees, and insects, and plants were filled with the Divine. The best I can describe it – is as though seeing with 'new eyes.' Every butterfly created a deep joy in me to witness its existence. Every flower filled me with peace. I had never felt like this before. This began to reveal the teachings of Hinduism and other spiritual paths of my past, as a concrete experience.

How did I get to this point? My path was for me, that I'm certain. Each step along the way got me here. But also, specific teachings of Dr. Masters put into daily practice (spiritual affirmation being a key factor) as well as the guided meditations of his on the subject of 'Heavenly Contact,' truly benefited me in achieving this feeling of 'oneness' with all of creation. – B.W.

. . . True spiritual teachers know that only the all-knowing within oneself can provide ultimate enlightenment. Only Universal Consciousness, Mind, Spirit, or God within oneself can provide the ultimate spiritual experience. Dr. Paul Leon Masters is proven to be a true spiritual teacher . . . – D.Z.

I am new to Dr. Masters' work, but not to the field of metaphysics, psychology and the paranormal. I found that Dr. Masters' work is refreshing. In all of my research, study, and experience, I have discovered that what he is teaching is indeed important and the most valuable. The journey begins within . . . – D.K.

. . . I could watch Dr. Masters' lectures for hours every day . . . well I sometimes do!! Such an inspirational, beautiful soul and such a blessing to have found him!! – H. R.

I have studied under Dr. Masters personally when he was living. One of the few people that ACTUALLY knows what he is talking about. – C. R.

Thank you for the comprehensive ultra-valuable wisdom. - K.M.

I appreciate Dr. Masters' daily message and his mini consults. I'm reaching higher and moving forward and in doing so, helping others in their own quest for wholeness. Thank you for making it possible to find applicable practices for my daily life and for being an authentic voice in a time when one is needed. – FB Post

A wealth of information that has opened many doors for me. – L.G.C.

I can't believe the change that has come over me. Everything has changed in the twinkling of an eye. My relationships with family, friends, and clients have all changed for the better, my perception and awareness has opened up overnight, and my intuition has opened up, giving me what was missing from my life. I know my intuition is going to get stronger by the day. Your work is Pure Light. – T.S.

Whoever created this program is, without doubt, walking in the light and direct contact with the higher mind of God. – E.G.

DEDICATION

Affirmations are a cornerstone of Dr. Masters' teachings, whether in his Weekly Inspirational Lectures or the coursework for the worldwide universities he founded: the University of Metaphysics and the University of Sedona. This collection of affirmations within this book stand as a testament to Dr. Masters' belief in the power of positive thinking and using affirmations to advance and enlighten all areas of the human experience and to elevate human potential.

Dr. Masters' vast experience in metaphysical counseling, his dedication to mental-spiritual growth, and his in-depth exploration of higher consciousness has made him an inspirationally dynamic and eloquent writer and speaker. It was always Dr. Masters' intention to release an affirmation book that would empower and uplift the lives of many. The release of this powerful book is especially timely, as we navigate today's unprecedented and challenging times.

It is with great pleasure that we publish Dr. Masters' second book, *Spiritual Mind Power Affirmations,* in dedication to its author and in honor of his legacy as a pioneer, teacher, and caretaker of the study and exploration of metaphysics.

— International Metaphysical Ministry

CONTENTS

INTRODUCTION

Over the course of his lifetime of service, Dr. Paul Leon Masters presented a large number of inspirational lectures during his Sunday services. Almost all of them began with a meditation or healing treatment, after which he presented a teaching that included an affirmation. Many listeners commented on the healing transmission of his lectures and later asked for copies of the affirmation sheets.

Affirmations are positive thought statements with a spiritual or mystical base, worded in such a manner as to keep our conscious mind attuned to our higher God Mind. It is interesting to note that affirmations can be considered mystical prayer if they have been inspired and intuitively created by God's Presence within you.

If you have ever been moved to write down an affirmative thought, particularly one that seemed to come from somewhere beyond your intellect, the chances are that it was inspired by God's Presence at the center of your mind. An affirmation is a statement of truth that is based on spiritual truth.

Affirmations create Oneness with the God Power in your mind, and allow the God Power to flow through and into your daily activities. Words that you use in affirmations must have real meaning to you if your affirmations are to work effectively.

Affirmations are used to keep the conscious or mental part of the mind attuned and working with the inner truth of God's Presence. Used daily, they have dramatically changed the lives of thousands of people. They may be practiced aloud, or in the silence of what I term affirmative meditation.

A person may be more receptive to receiving intuitive direction from God if they maintain a conscious state of mind that is open to receive. An affirmation, such as the following example, can help to maintain the conscious mind in a receptive state:

The love of the Universe for me, in God's Mind within me, vibrates the magnetic power of love through me, this day.

To prepare yourself to be in a receptive state, *repeat the affirmations to yourself at least once daily, preferably spoken, if possible.* After speaking or thinking each affirmation, close your eyes momentarily and feel that the reality of the affirmation is traveling into every level of your mind while merging and synthesizing with the center; the Presence, Universal Mind, or God within you.

The conscious use of these affirmations will affect your immediate conscious attitude during the day, making you more positive. At the same time, it will condition a subconscious acceptance of a new, successful you, which will make it easier for your God Mind to channel through your subconscious the intuition and power you need to make your life successful.

The content of this book consists of the affirmations that Dr. Masters presented in his inspirational lectures. As you connect with the affirmations in this book, should you care to deepen your awareness on a particular point, you may search the www.metaphysics.com website for the recorded lecture under the same title.

May the light of God's Presence within you guide others to awaken to the very same presence within themselves.

Dr. Paul L. Masters, Founder
International Metaphysical Ministry
University of Metaphysics
University of Sedona

Spiritual Mind Power Affirmations

Practical, Mystical, and Spiritual Inspiration Applied to Your Life

ABUNDANCE
AND
PROSPERITY

ACHIEVING LASTING SECURITY

LASTING: I recognize that the only thing that is really lasting is eternity itself, and that if I am to find anything lasting, it must be eternal.

ETERNAL SELFHOOD: I recognize that there is a part of my beingness which is eternal or the Christ part of my mind where my soul and God are in oneness.

ETERNAL BEINGNESS: I recognize that I am one in Christ's mind with God's eternal presence.

UNCHANGING: I recognize that ultimate, unchanging security is to be found in my oneness with the unchanging eternal security that is God.

POWER: I recognize that the Christ/God part of me is all powerful and has total power over the security of my body, mind, and soul in this lifetime and through eternity.

MEDITATION: Through my daily practice of meditation I contact my eternal Christ Mind/God Oneness, which fills my beingness with security in difficult times as well as good times.

VISUALIZATION: I visualize or imagine the entirety of my body on a spiritual level as being filled with God's Light Presence of lasting, eternal security.

ETERNAL MOMENT: I live in the eternal moment of now that is God's measure of time where my security is lasting and eternal.

RECOGNITION: I recognize that my material, emotional and health security are under the power of the lasting, eternal presence of God within me.

HOLISTICALLY LABOR LESS - HAVE MORE

LABORING LESS: I accept and acknowledge that the key to laboring less and having more is to use my mind more and my body less.

USING BODY LESS: I accept and understand that using my body less means not only physical activity, but also the time my body spends at any type of work, including mental.

HOLISTICALLY: Holistically means that to have more while having to labor less is as a result of also engaging God's Presence of Universal Mind and Spirit to intuitively direct the surface part of my mind as to what to do to labor less and have more.

WILL: I let go and release my personal will to God's Will and Presence within me knowing that by so doing, God's Power and Wisdom work through my surface mind for me to have more with less labor.

CREATIVE IDEAS: I affirm that God's Presence at the center of consciousness within me is constantly providing my surface mind with creative ideas I can use to labor less and have more.

CHOOSING LEADERSHIP: In whatever I choose to do in my life according to God's Will for my life or my soul's purpose, I will accept a position of leadership knowing that leadership can bring rewards of laboring less and having more.

LEADERSHIP: I understand that leadership is not limited to management or owning a company and can also mean being the pace setter or leader in the arts, music, or any number of areas in the commercial world, government, and so on.

ULTIMATE LEADERSHIP: I acknowledge that my life is under the directives of God's Presence within me that leads my mind daily to accomplish and have more by laboring less.

INCREASING YOUR INCOME IN THE NEW YEAR

ATTITUDE: I have a positive attitude about having more income in the New Year based on God's Power within me to make it so.

SOURCE ACKNOWLEDGEMENT: I acknowledge that my ultimate source for more income in the New Year is God's Presence within me.

RELEASE PAST LACK: I totally release, from all levels of my mind, any and all thoughts of past lack, and that I no longer consider myself lacking in funds made possible through God as my Source.

SELF-IMAGE: Daily, I maintain a self-image of myself as being one with God's Presence, and that God shares universal wealth with me.

MEDITATION: Through my daily practice of meditation, I open the intuitive channels of my mind to be intuitively directed by God's Presence within me to increase my income in the New Year.

CREATIVITY: Through God's intuition gained through meditation, creative prospering ideas are entering my conscious awareness throughout the New Year.

ADAPTABILITY: In a rapidly changing world, I draw upon God's unlimited consciousness to provide me with the adaptability to be able to make changes quickly to increase my income in the New Year.

CONSCIOUS COOPERATION: Daily, I am in conscious cooperation with God's Will for my life, knowing that as God's Will manifests through me, I, in turn, will manifest increased income in the New Year.

ALREADY SO: I accept, totally and completely, that increased income in the New Year is already so in the mind of God for me, and so it is!

KEYS TO SUCCESS IN TODAY'S WORLD

CHRIST MINDED: Like Jesus, I am Christ Minded by recognizing my oneness with God's Presence within me which provides what I need in an ever-changing world.

GOD'S WILL: The surface me draws upon the all knowingness, love, and healing of God by turning over my personal will to God's Will, as I live each day in a rapidly changing world.

CENTERED: Every day I take a few moments several times to be centered in awareness on God's Presence within me.

FOCUSED: I go about my daily activities keeping focused on goals that God has established for me and do not allow myself to become distracted, knowing that in my own way, I am about God's business.

ADAPTABLE: In my oneness with God's Presence, I can readily adapt to new and changing conditions in today's world.

MULTI-TALENTED: As God is capable of all things, God's Presence within me provides me with multi-talents to function in today's world.

MEDITATION: I take time daily to meditate on God's Presence within me, knowing that my oneness with God's Presence is the ultimate key to my real needs in whatever is taking place in the world today.

INTUITION: Through my daily meditations I am intuitively guided by God's Presence within me to meet my real needs by living God's Will for my life.

CREATIVITY: Through God's creative presence within me, I bring forth creative ideas to meet the challenges of my place in an ever-changing world.

SACREDNESS: I hold my life Sacred for in Christ Minded awareness I am about my Father's (God's) business and in so doing I am blessed and in turn am a blessing to others.

MYSTICAL SECRETS OF PROSPERING

SEEK FIRST: To have all things added to my life I seek first the higher consciousness of God's Presence or the kingdom of heaven within me.

MEDITATION: Through my daily practice of meditation, I open my conscious awareness to God's Presence, who in turn provides the intuition, sensing, and guidance necessary to prosper.

PERSONAL WILL TO GOD'S WILL: I daily turn over my personal will to God's Will, for it is God's Presence, wisdom, power, and creativeness that is prospering itself.

ALREADY SO: I recognize that whatever can be already is, in a moment of eternal time including prospering.

CHOOSING: Through my oneness with God's eternal presence I choose prospering as my experience of one eternal moment.

I AM: In oneness with God's Presence I need not try to attract anything, for I already am all that I could seek to attract, and in being all things I am already prosperous.

UNSEEN: In the consciousness of God and the Universe, God's Will is in motion in the unseen realm of spirit to energize my prospering.

ATTITUDE: My attitude is one of positiveness about prospering due to my oneness with God's Presence established through meditation and a releasing of my personal will to God's Will daily.

POWERIZING WEALTH IN YOUR NEW YEAR

MEDITATION: Through my daily practice of mediation in this New Year, I contact my ultimate source for wealth, the God power presence at the innermost center of my mind.

VISUALIZATION: I daily take a few moments to visualize or imagine the interior of my body filled with God's Light Presence in and through which wealth-creating ideas are born and directed into my conscious awareness.

WILL: In and throughout this New Year I give up my personal will and yield it to the all-powerful will of God within me that I may be powerized to wealth by the same will that created the Universe.

IDENTIFICATION: In Christ Mindedness, I identify my innermost reality as being in a state of eternal oneness with God, and thus, co-owner of all the wealth that is, with a sufficient portion individualized to my human life.

FIRST PRIORITY: I recognize that my first priority as I start a New Year, and throughout it, is to seek God's heavenly consciousness at the center of my mind, knowing that through such contact all else that I need will be added to me.

WEALTH IMAGE: I affirm throughout all levels of my mind that I experience a wealthy way of life through the grace that is the power of God working in and through me in this New Year and through eternity.

OUTER/INNER WEALTH BALANCE: I recognize that true, absolute wealth is a balance between the temporary wealth of this earthly life and the lasting wealth and inner treasure of eternal life or my soul's oneness with God.

PROSPERING IN HARD TIMES

OPPORTUNITIES: I regard hard times as an atmosphere that stimulates new opportunities through which I may prosper.

REALISM: At all times I am realistic about hard times, but not pessimistic about opportunities to prosper.

DOORWAYS: I recognize that as some doors to prospering close, new doors to prospering open to me through God's Presence working in my life.

SUCCESS ENERGY: I vibrate success energy, even in the hardest of times, which attracts prospering to me.

INTUITIVE GUIDANCE: Through my inner oneness with God's Presence, I am intuitively guided as to how to prosper during hard times.

CREATIVE IDEAS: Through my inner oneness with God's Presence, creative ideas for prospering in hard times flow into my mind continually.

VISUALIZATION: Daily, I take a few moments to visualize or imagine the entire interior of my body filled with God's creative light Christ energy in which creative ideas that I may use to prosper are born.

MEDITATION: Through my daily practice of meditation, I establish and maintain a oneness with God's Presence that provides me with all I need to prosper, even during hard times.

CHOICE: There are always people who find ways to prosper during hard times, and through the power, wisdom, creativity, and will of God's Presence within me, I choose to be one of those prosperous persons.

PROSPERING THROUGH CREATIVE IDEA SOURCING

ONE CREATIVE IDEA: All it takes is just one creative idea to prosper me, and that creative idea exists within me now in the presence of God within me, the source of all creativeness.

MEDITATION: Through my daily practice of meditation, I establish and maintain contact with the innermost center of consciousness within me, the mind of God, universal intelligence, the source of all creative ideas.

VISUALIZATION: Daily, I take a few moments to visualize or imagine God light energy containing one or more creative ideas moving upward from the frontal part of my chest area to my head area, providing me with the creative thoughts necessary to prosper.

ATTUNEMENT OF WILL: Daily, I give up my personal will and its limited intellect to the unlimited will of the Universe, or God, containing all creative ideas.

SPONTANEOUS APPEARANCE: I understand that creative ideas suddenly appear in my mind without any intellectual reasoning.

GOD ALREADY KNOWS: The God part of my mind already knows exactly which creative idea needs to be known by the conscious level of my mind to experience more prospering.

TOTAL PROSPERING: In my oneness and wholeness with God, I experience prospering as a whole person and, thus, love and health in abundance as well as materially.

SOUL'S PURPOSE: I affirm daily that God's creative prospering ideas are in tune with my soul's purpose in this lifetime and at this time in my life.

ONENESS: I am in God and God is in me and thus, all creative ideas that exist in God exist in me!

THE ECONOMY, GOD, AND YOU

CHANGELESS: The presence of God within me is eternally changeless, secure, whole, and complete.

ONENESS: God's Presence working through the Christ Mind within me knows exactly what I have real need of before I even ask, if I have been practicing Christ Mindedness daily.

MEDITATION: Through my Christ Minded practice of mediation on God's Presence within me every day, my conscious mind is directed to fulfill my material and worldly needs.

WILL: Through my Christ Mind practice of giving up my personal will to God's Will daily, God's Will supplies and guides me to my material and worldly needs.

VISUALIZATION: Every day I take a few moments to visualize or imagine that the Christ Mind light filling my body, on a spiritual level, merges energy factors and guidance bringing about the fulfilling of my material and worldly needs.

OTHERS: Daily, I take a few moments to declare that God's Presence in others is materializing and guiding whoever is open to receive physically, materially, mentally, and spiritually.

REACTION AND ACTION: I understand it is human to react to financial and material letdowns and divine to let go to God's Presence within me to take action regarding my needs.

PROSPERING: Through practicing Christ Mindedness daily, God's Presence provides me with creative prosperity ideas I may use to prosper, even in the midst of hard economic times.

DAILY ATTITUDE: God knows my real needs and supplies them.

TOTAL WEALTH: MATERIALLY, MENTALLY, AND SPIRITUALLY

TWO CHRISTIANITIES: I understand that there are two Christianities, the outer for the mass of souls as yet unable to comprehend the subtleties and complexities of the simplest truth of all, and the other secret Christianity of the Disciples, made known to only a few, who, when ready to enter into the mysteries of knowingness or Christ Mind Consciousness, have it inwardly revealed to them.

TOTAL WEALTH: I recognize that my prospering materially, mentally, and spiritually is a result of my living in Christ Mind Consciousness as guided intuitively by Universal Consciousness or God.

CHRIST: I recognize that the word Christ refers to the state of consciousness or mind level within me here, and my existence is in an eternal state of oneness with Universal Consciousness or God.

PRIORITY: I recognize that my first priority in life is to live in Christ Mind Consciousness that I may be inwardly connected to Universal Consciousness or God to be in charge of my thinking and feeling nature, that I may receive total wealth according to God's wisdom and will for the enrichment of my soul in this life and beyond.

SOURCE: I recognize that my real source for a life of total wealth comes from the Universal Consciousness of God within me, channeled through the Christ Mind intuitive awareness active in me.

KNOWING: I recognize that total wealth is achieved, not through mortally thinking something into existence, but by Christ Mind knowing, intuitively guided by Universal Consciousness or God as to both thinking and feeling.

WEALTH GOALS: I recognize that total wealth is achieved when my outer thinking and feeling processes are intuitively guided by knowing what my goals are, established not by mortal mind level limitations, but by the all-knowing universal God consciousness within me channeled through Christ Mindedness.

WORLDLY WEALTH: I recognize that worldly wealth can be achieved in making money and material possessions the number one priority or focus of the outer mortal mind, but that in so doing, connection with universal consciousness or total wealth is almost impossible and can lead to unhappiness, emptiness within, and escapisms with and in spite of worldly wealth.

LASTING WEALTH: I recognize that anything lasting must be eternal, so I seek as my first priority to be one with the eternal part of me as the lasting treasure which provides for me in this life and beyond it through eternity.

CLEANSING: I recognize that the mortal levels of consciousness within me must be cleansed of negative karma, trauma, thinking, and feeling or I will be in conflict with Christ Mindedness and, thus, block the intuitive channeling of universal God consciousness to achieve total wealth.

WILL: I daily give up my personal will and corresponding mortal thinking and feeling to the will of universal God consciousness which provides me with the knowing to live in total wealth.

REALITY: I recognize that while there is a physical abundance of all things for all people, that only a few achieve total wealth, for the universal God consciousness only provides to its creations the power inherent in knowingness that they are prepared to experience to not destroy themselves and others through a mortally obstructed view or reality.

WEALTH PRODUCING CREATIVE IDEAS

CREATIVE IDEAS: I recognize that all it takes to produce wealth is just one creative idea as simple as a paper clip or bobby pin.

SOURCE: I understand that all original wealth-producing creative ideas come from one source, or God's Presence, at the center of the human mind.

ALREADY PRESENT: I understand that an enormous abundance of wealth-producing creative ideas are already present at the God center of my own mind.

THE RIGHT ONE: I recognize that the exact, right, wealth producing, creative idea exists for where my life currently is in the God center of my mind.

SOUL'S PURPOSE: I declare that throughout my life that I become aware of the right wealth-producing, creative ideas that are in total accord for the spiritual purpose of my soul in this lifetime.

WILL: I turn over my personal will to God's Will daily, knowing that by so doing, God's Presence in me can better communicate wealth-producing, creative ideas to my conscious mind's awareness.

MEDITATION: I am aware that through my daily practice of meditation I establish and maintain a flow of thought energy to better bring to my conscious mind's awareness wealth-producing, creative ideas.

MOTIVATION: My motivation for wealth-producing ideas is that a portion of the wealth produced may be used to help people who are in financial or material need; to discover how to bring forth wealth-producing, creative ideas from the God source center within their own minds.

YOU HAVE WHAT IT TAKES

EVERYTHING: I've got what it takes to be loved, healthy, prosperous, happy; everything.

HOW AND WHY: I've got what it takes because in absolute spiritual truth the ultimate life in my body is God with all power, wisdom, love, and healing to do what it takes within and through me.

IDENTITY: I identify totally and completely with the presence of God within my body as the doer of all that needs to be done in my life, according to God's purpose for me in this lifetime.

MIND: The surface level of my conscious mind yields itself daily to the Universal Mind Consciousness of God so that my conscious awareness has exactly what it takes in love, health, prospering; everything.

WILL: Daily I give up my surface personal will to the real will contained in my body or God's Will with the universal will power that has what it takes to create the Universe and, thus, most certainly everything in my life.

MEDITATION: Through my daily practice of meditation I give up my personal sense of presence to the presence of God at the innermost center of consciousness within me that contains all that it takes for me in matters of love, health, prospering; everything.

ENERGIZED: The power, will, knowingness, healing, and love of God's Presence working through me energizes my body, mind, and soul to accomplish and succeed in my life and with my life.

YOUR POTENTIALS IN LOVE, CAREER, AND LIFE

DEFINING POTENTIAL: I understand that I can choose either the potentials to be found only in the limited personal ego part of myself or the potentials that are part of Christ level of my mind, one with the divine potentials of God.

CHOICE OF WILLS: I give up my personal will to the will of God for my life, knowing that as I do, I open myself to having God bring forth my potentials and provide the energy and wisdom for them to become a physical life reality.

MEDITATION: Through my daily practice of meditation, I open my conscious mind to God for an awareness of my potentials for this lifetime and the wisdom to realize them.

INTUITION: Through my daily practice of meditation, the intuitive directions of God flow into my conscious mind, guiding me to an achieving of my God-given potentials.

SOURCE CREDIT: I give credit for all my potentials to the source from which they originated; God's Presence at the center of consciousness within me.

VISUALIZATION: Whatever potential I am striving for, I take a few moments daily to visualize myself as living and enjoying that achieved potential.

LOVE: Daily, I turn over my soul to God's spirit of love within me which fills me with love sufficient to achieve my potential for love in this lifetime.

CAREER: In my inner oneness with God's Presence, I am unlimited in my career potentials.

LIFE: In all areas of my life, my body, mind, and soul are activated by God's Presence of potentials.

CHANNELING: I recognize that all my potentials are part of the divine attributes of God within me seeking expression.

CHRIST
CONSCIOUSNESS

CELEBRATING THE MYSTERIES OF CHRIST, THE RESURRECTION, AND YOU

REALIZATION: All events in the life of Jesus symbolize inner events in the awakening and resurrection of Christ Consciousness in me.

RESURRECTION: I realize that the physical resurrection of Christ symbolizes the resurrection of Christ Mind Consciousness in me.

CHRIST MIND CONSCIOUSNESS: I recognize that Christ Mind Consciousness is that part of my mind where my mortal presence and Universal Mind, or God, are as one presence.

MEDITATION: Through my daily practice of meditation I resurrect Christ Mind Consciousness within myself.

RESURRECTION VISUALIZATION: Daily, I take a few moments to mentally visualize or imagine that either the figure of Jesus, representing Christ Consciousness in me, or a Christ light, is ascending upward within me from the trunk of my body rising upward into my head and out through the top of it into whatever infinity may be.

GRAVE CLOTHES REMOVAL: Throughout my mind, I remove the grave clothes of mortal life death to be resurrected into the light of Christ Mind Consciousness in my awareness, thoughts, and feelings.

RESURRECTED LIVING: I am daily under the influence of the risen Christ Mind Consciousness resurrected in me.

IDENTITY: My resurrected identity is lived in onement with Christ/God/Universal Mind/Spirit Consciousness.

ONEMENT: In my resurrected Christ Mind Consciousness, I am in onement with God's love, health, creativity, fulfillment, and happiness throughout my body, mind, and soul.

CHRIST'S RESURRECTION AND YOURS
FROM WORLDLY CONCERNS

LIFE EVENTS: I realize that every physical event in the life of Jesus symbolizes an event of Christ Consciousness within me, including resurrection.

DEATH SYMBOL: I realize that the physical death of Jesus on the cross symbolizes the death of mortal consciousness within me.

MORTAL CONSCIOUSNESS: I understand that mortal consciousness is that which is personal under the illusions and limitations of outer sense impressions from the physical world.

CHRIST CONSCIOUSNESS: I understand that Christ Consciousness is that part of my mind that is an eternal state of oneness with God's Consciousness at the innermost center of my mental beingness.

RESURRECTION: I understand that resurrection, as it affects me, is rising above my mind's mortal consciousness with its illusions and limitations to Christ Consciousness with contact to God's realities and unlimited resources.

CHRIST RISEN: Every day I declare that Christ Consciousness is risen in me, raising me to awareness through which I am able to see clearly in my mind and Spirit exactly what I should do with conditions and circumstances in my physical life.

MEDIATION: Through my daily practice of meditation, I establish and maintain contact with the presence of Christ Consciousness within my mind.

VISUALIZATION: I daily take a few moments to visualize or imagine the entire interior of my body filled with Christ Light Consciousness.

I AM: I am, consciously or unconsciously, resurrected from mortal consciousness to Christ conscious oneness with God which provides me with the wisdom, will, positiveness, healing, hope, and love to rise in Christ Consciousness to what is necessary to outgrow, deal with, and overcome physical life circumstances and conditions.

EXPERIENCING GOD'S PRESENCE

MYSTICAL EXPERIENCE: I understand that mystical experience is the actual, direct, extra-sensory experience of universal God consciousness light, in oneness with and to the exclusion of all else, yet in merger with all.

POSSIBILITY: I understand that it is possible for anyone to have mystical experience, but that it is God's Presence that chooses when, and that it could be me.

MYSTICS: I understand that people down through the ages who have had direct mystical experience of God's Presence are known as mystics.

PRIORITY: I understand that the direct mystical experience of God's Presence is far more possible if I make such an experience the number one priority in my life.

EGO: I understand that the only thing that is between me and direct mystical experience of God's Presence is personal ego energy controlling my awareness and, hence, will do all possible to reduce or eliminate its influence in my consciousness.

ONENESS: Every day I declare that the only true, ultimate life that is in my body is God's life, Spirit, mind presence.

INDIVIDUALIZED EXPRESSION: Daily, I recognize that I am an individualized expression of God's spirit mind presence.

SOUL'S PURPOSE: As an individualized expression of God, my purpose for being created is, in fact, God's purpose.

MEDITATION: By living my life in my mind with an awareness of the previous affirmations, my conscious mind is in tune with, ready to receive, and mystically experience God's Presence.

FROM EGO MIND TO GOD CONSCIOUSNESS

NOT: I am not my social security number, driver's license, credit cards, political party affiliate of any earthly country in the physical dimension.

NOT: I am not the illusions of time or space, nor any physical measurement.

NOT: I am not human, animal, or mineral.

NOT: I am not a human man or woman.

NOT: I am not of any race or combination of a race of people.

NOT: I am not human thought, human feelings, or human beingness.

I AM LIGHT: I am universal light body energy, containing all things while within all existence.

I AM TIMELESS: I am timeless without beginning or ending.

I AM: I am simultaneously All, beyond All, as All.

ILLUSIONS AND REALITY: I am All that seems to be and All that really is.

I AM: I am pure consciousness, pure mind, pure Spirit.

MEDITATION: Through my daily practice of meditation, I reawaken to the eternal reality of my ultimate Christ selfhood in God.

HAVING A CHRIST MIND

CHRIST MIND: Christ Mind is that part of the innermost center of my mind where my personal sense of consciousness and the universal consciousness of God exist as one presence.

IDENTITY: I recognize that my ultimate identity is one with the eternal presence of God or a state of Christ Mind Consciousness.

MEDITATION: Through my daily practice of meditation, I establish a connection with God's universal consciousness, which provides me with Christ Mindedness.

WILL: Daily, I give up my personal and mortal mind consciousness to God's Will channeled through the Christed mind within me.

RELEASE: I am constantly releasing what needs to be done in my life from the Christ Mind in me to universal God consciousness at the center of my beingness.

INTUITION: My Christ Mind Consciousness is under the intuitive guidance of universal God consciousness within me.

AWARENESS: In Christ Mind awareness I am aware of both the short-term and long-term results of my actions.

DOING: I accept that in Christ Mindedness I am aware that God's Presence within me is the true doer of all accomplished good in my life; past, present, and future.

CREATIVITY: I accept that the Christ Mind within me becomes aware of creative ideas coming from universal God consciousness in me, which is the source for ideas with which to improve my life.

PERSPECTIVE: I am in this world but my Christ Mind exists in a higher state of consciousness, one with God's Universal Mind.

HOW TO BE GOD GUIDED

PRIORITY: I realize that to be God guided, I must be as close to God as possible and therefore make my relationship to God the number one priority in my life.

DEDICATION: I dedicate my body, mind, and soul to God's Presence within me, for the greater my dedication, the more God guidance I receive.

WILL: I give up my personal will to God's Will and thus, increase God's guidance as my soul's purpose for this lifetime is more readily achieved.

NEGATIVITY RELEASE: I release all stored up negative energy in my body, mind, and soul to the sublimating light of God's healing light within me, knowing that negative energy forms an internal blockage to the positive energy of God's guidance.

GOD'S THINKING: I am more open to receive God's guidance when I think more like God, which is thinking about everyone's needs, not just my own.

CHRIST LIGHT VISUALIZATION: I visualize the entire interior of my body filled with the light of Christ Consciousness or that part of onement with God where I may receive God's guidance.

MEDITATION: Through my daily practice of meditation, I establish and maintain a pipeline flow of thought between Christ Mind Consciousness and God, through which I may receive God's guidance.

LIVING YOUR DAILY LIFE IN
CHRIST MIND CONSCIOUSNESS

AWAKENING: Upon awakening from sleep each day, I take a few moments to dedicate the day to God's Presence, will, and consciousness that direct me from within myself.

MID-DAY RENEWAL: At the mid-point of my daily activities, I dedicate the remainder of the day to God's renewing energy and peace that exists within my soul/mind/body beingness.

EVENING GRATITUDE: At the conclusion of my day's activities, I dedicate all that has happened to God's Presence, giving God credit for all good and releasing all that seems negative or unfavorable to God's healing light presence within me.

SLEEP ATTUNEMENT: Just before I sense that I am about to go to sleep each day, I take a moment to declare that during sleep, God's Presence is healing and renewing me while planting guidance thoughts just below the conscious level of my mind that I will become aware of during my waking activities.

MEDITATION: I recognize that the time I spend daily in a state of meditation is the most important part of my day, for it maintains or reestablishes my connection to God's Presence at the innermost center of consciousness within me.

VISUALIZATION: Periodically, as I am about my daily activities, I visualize or imagine that the entire interior of my body, at a spiritual level of consciousness, is filled with God's Presence as light which I recognize as my ultimate, absolute Christ self-reality, one with God.

INTUITIVE GUIDANCE: God's Presence within me as my ultimate Christ self-guides and directs my thoughts and feelings as I go about my daily activities.

CHRIST SELF/GOD DOER: At the beginning, and periodically as I go about my daily activities, I declare that it is God's Presence, will, love, and power working through the Christ-self part of my mind and body that is the actual doer of all that is being done and accomplished.

MY DAILY LIFE: I recognize that my daily life is going about God's business (meaning releasing my personal will to God's Will) as God working through my Christ Mind self and body goes about taking care of my outer physical world business, releasing me from the anxiety and stress of doing through personal selfhood.

LIVING YOUR LIFE FREE OF LIMITATIONS

DEFINING LIMITATION: From a perspective of ultimate self-truth, I define limitation as an illusion of personal selfhood or separation of identity from the ultimate presence of God.

ULTIMATE SELF: I accept that my ultimate self is Christ Consciousness or in eternal mind onement with the unlimited presence of God within me.

MEDITATION: Through my daily practice of meditation, I establish and maintain contact with the unlimited part of my Christ/God self.

VISUALIZATION: At least once daily, I take a few moments to visualize or imagine that I am part of the unlimited infinite Christ light body of God's Presence within me.

RELEASE: I release my personal self-beliefs and corresponding limitations to the unlimited presence of God within me.

MIND FREEDOM: I declare that my mind can be one with God's mind which knows all freedom, for it is all things with power within all creation.

SOUL FREEDOM: Through God's Presence within my very soul, God's freedom to be is a part of my inner most nature, my soul, to be free of illusionary limitations.

HOLISTIC FREEDOM: Through my oneness with God's Presence within me, I have an unlimited freedom to express holistically through my body, my mind, and soul.

FOCUSING: If ever I start to feel limited, I catch myself or mind and re-focus on the Christ conscious oneness with the unlimited presence and freedom of God at the center of my beingness.

MIND CONNECTING WITH GOD'S ATTRIBUTES

PURPOSE: I understand that the purpose of mind connecting with God is to bring forth God's attributes from within me into manifesting in my physical life.

MEDITATION: I understand that my daily practice of meditation is the key to connecting my mind to God's mind and thus God's attributes.

PERSONAL EGO: I understand that I must set aside my personal ego, whose energies tend to repress God's attributes, by daily turning over my personal will to God's Will.

ABUNDANCE: By connecting with God's mind in which everything is contained, I connect with the energy of abundance which manifest through me and draws abundance to me.

POWER: By connecting with God's mind, my body, mind, and soul are energized by the primal light energy source of God's Presence.

WISDOM: By connecting with God's mind, the eternal wisdom of the ages illuminates my thoughts with thoughts that I can use to improve my life as well as others.

HEALTH: By connecting with God's mind, the perfection of God's Presence flows into and through my body, maintaining good health or restoring health throughout my body.

LOVE: By connecting with God's mind, I connect with the source of love in the Universe and it flows in and through me to others, and in so doing attracts love back to me.

OTHERS: By connecting with God's mind and thus, God's love, I let forgiveness, understanding, compassion, and support flow through me to others, that they may feel and experience God's caring.

MYSTERIES OF CHRIST CONSCIOUSNESS

FIRST MANIFESTATION: I understand that Christ Light Consciousness is the first manifestation of unmanifest Spirit or God ("The only begotten son of God" - Bible Reference).

LIGHT: I understand that Christ Consciousness exists as an infinite light field.

CENTER: I understand that Christ Light Consciousness exists in all creations, both animate and inanimate; the physical energy world; and other energy worlds of a non-physical nature.

FILTER: I understand that Christ Light Consciousness acts as a filter or filters through the consciousness or Spirit or God.

REACHING GOD: I understand that to reach God's Presence or Spirit, I must enter Christ Light Consciousness, which is one with God's unmanifest Spirit ("No man cometh unto the Father, except through me" - Bible Reference).

CO-EXISTENCE: I understand that Christ Light Consciousness and unmanifest God/Spirit Consciousness co-exist in a state of light within darkness, and darkness within light ("The father and I are one" - Bible Reference).

HUMAN CONSCIOUSNESS: I understand that, whether or not in every person's mind, Christ Light Consciousness exists, as entry contacts to God's Consciousness of Spirit ("Let the mind be in you that was in Christ Jesus" - Bible Reference).

ENTRANCE: I understand that to enter into the heavenly awareness of Christ Light Consciousness, and thus God's Presence, I must set aside my personal will in favor of God's Will, and become still enough through meditation to know or experience God's spirit ("Peace, be still and know the I am" - Bible Reference).

MYSTICAL ONENESS – THE KEY TO LIFE'S REWARDS

DEFINING: I understand that mystical oneness is oneness with God and All that is.

MEDITATION: Through my daily practice of meditation, I am able to establish and maintain an inner mind state of Christ conscious oneness with God.

OTHERS: Through my Christ conscious oneness with God, I am able to feel a oneness with others who contain the same God Presence within them.

VISUALIZATION: I take a few moments daily to visualize or imagine that the interior of my body, on a spiritual level, is filled with God's Light Presence. which gives me a state of oneness with the same God Light Presence in others.

NATURE: As God's Presence is in all manifestations of nature, I sense, feel, and am one with all the beauty seen in nature.

SUPPLY: I recognize that through my oneness with God, which is all things and creates and controls all things of earth and heaven, that whatever I need in life, according to God's purpose for my soul in this lifetime, is supplied.

HEALTH: In my oneness with God's perfection and wholeness living as the life force within me, that I am one in body, mind, and soul, with good health and healing.

LOVE: Through my oneness with God's Presence within me, whose nature is love, I connect with God's nature in others, attracting love to me.

HEALTH: In oneness with God, others, and the Universe, I am unlimited in what I am and can be.

SECRETS OF NEW BEGINNINGS

MEDITATION: Through my daily practice of meditation, I establish and maintain contact with the ultimate, on-going, creative, Universal Consciousness, Source, God; the power of eternal new beginnings.

VISUALIZATION: Daily, I take a few moments to visualize or imagine the interior of my body filled with the creative light of God's Presence from which all new beginnings originate before becoming physical manifestations.

RELEASE PAST: I give thanks to God's Presence within for all past good I have experienced and release this as well as all negativity of my past, that I may be in the universal God Mind energies of new beginnings.

WILL: I give up my personal will as God's Will is in charge of establishing exactly what new beginnings I should focus on.

CREATIVITY: Universal creating God conscious idea energies flow into the conscious level of my mind to initiate and complete new beginnings.

ETERNAL NOW: Whatever new beginnings God consciousness places in my conscious mind is already so, already a reality, already happened in universal consciousness of the mind of God.

EMPOWERMENT: I dwell in God and God in me whose nature to create new beginnings is individualized in me to empower my body, mind, and soul to be successful in creating new beginnings in my physical life and beyond.

REAL PRAYER WORKS - HOW AND WHY

VARIETY: I understand that there are many forms of prayer, but that the highest or real prayer is meditational as it was taught through the Christ Mind in Jesus for those who could understand.

MEDITATION: Meditation is real prayer because it provides a oneness of presence with God, whose power, creativity, and intuitive guidance is the source for praying successfully.

GOD KNOWS: In the New Testament it states, "Your Father knoweth what you have need of before you ask;" and therefore in reality I need not use asking prayer, but rather meditation to be open to God's Presence as my source.

SECRET: By praying to the Father God which seeith in secret (within the higher Heavenly consciousness within me), the Father God shall reward me openly according to what God knows to be my greatest need.

WILL: To gain full or more complete entrance into the Kingdom of Heavenly God consciousness within me, I declare every day of my life that not my personal will, but God's Will be done through me.

SOURCE: From the smallest to the largest good I experience in human life, I recognize that it is by the grace of God's Presence within me and through my inner oneness with God's Presence and will gained through my daily practice of meditational prayer.

LIGHT: The light of God creates in and through me.

SUPPLY: God within me knows what I truly have need of before I ask and is supplying it.

SUCCESSFUL PRAYER: As God supplies exactly what I really have need of, all my meditational prayer or inner communion with God is successful.

YOGA OF THE CHRIST MIND KIND

RAJA YOGA: I work successfully with the inner energy/matter of my mind, guided intuitively by God's Presence to find and awaken to God's Universal Mind/Spirit.

MEDITATION: Through my daily practice of meditation, I achieve the relaxation and concentration necessary to make my mind one pointed to work with the inner energies of consciousness within me.

VRITTIS: Through God's Presence within me, I am intuitively guided in working with the inner energies (vrittis) of my mind that the color frequencies may be re-absorbed into light (Christ Consciousness) of Universal Mind/Spirit or God.

CHITTA: Through God's Presence within me, I am intuitively guided in working with the mind stuff (chitta) to turn mind forms into energies; and energies to color frequencies that may be re-absorbed into light (Christ Consciousness) of Universal Mind/Spirit or God.

WORKING WITH: Through deep meditational relaxation, the inner energies (vrittis) of my mind are slowed and stilled to the point where the color frequencies may be re-absorbed into light Christ Consciousness of Universal Mind/Spirit or God.

THIRD EYE: Through God's Presence intuitively guiding me, I work to still energy frequencies appearing as colors, shapes, and forms before my third eye, or inner sight of my forehead, or the whole interior of my head.

LIGHT: In meditation, I work to enlarge any light appearing in my third eye area by holding it steady in an inner gaze.

CHRIST MIND: I am one with the Christ Mind light of God's Presence, and I am intuitively led to achieve oneness with the Christ light, the doorway of consciousness to God's Presence.

YOUR DREAMS AS GOD'S GUIDANCE

NIGHTLY: I am aware that I dream and that whether I remember my dreams or not, God's Presence at the center of my mind is influencing my dreams for my physical, mental, and spiritual well-being.

SYMBOLS: I understand that most of the content of my dreams are symbols representing an associated reality in my thinking.

SYMBOL EXAMPLES: I understand, as an example, that death in a dream may symbolize death of old patterns of living, behavior or belief, or that birth may symbolize a newness to my way of life.

CURRENT EVALUATION: I understand that God's Presence may symbolically let my conscious, mortal self know what I have overcome in myself, or what I currently need to work on, or what I need to improve in the future.

SOMATIC: God's Presence within me that is aware of the health of my body may through my dream content inform me about the condition of my body health wise.

REPEATING DREAMS: I understand that repeating dreams are doing so because the awareness of what God is communicating has either not been accepted or understood by the conscious, personal ego part of the mind.

INTERPRETING: God's Presence at the center of my mind intuitively guides me to correctly interpret the symbols and meanings of my dreams.

COOPERATIVE DREAM TIME: I cooperate with God's Presence trying to inform me through my dreams, by declaring every night before falling asleep, that God is guiding me through the dreams I dream tonight and always.

YOU'RE PERFECT ALREADY - BEING IT

DEFINING PERFECTION: I understand that the spiritual defining of perfection is absolute beingness without need for change, the eternal or God.

DEFINING YOU: I accept that the real me of me is eternally one with the absolute perfection of God's Presence within me.

DEFINING - BEING IT: I understand that Being It means assuming and channeling the perfection of God's Presence according to my soul's purpose at this time in this lifetime.

BIBLICAL REFERENCE: "Be ye perfect even as your Father (God), in heaven is perfect."

GOD'S LOCATION: The Kingdom of God or Heaven is at the innermost center of consciousness within me.

ONENESS: At the absolute spiritual level of my beingness, I am one with God and thus God's perfection.

GOD'S PERFECTION: I accept that God's perfection includes creativity, wisdom, love, healing, and power with which I am one.

MEDITATION: Through my daily practice of meditation, I establish and maintain contact with the perfection of all God's attributes within me.

BEING IT: Every day, I open my conscious mind to channel into my daily life the perfection that I already am due to my inner oneness with universal God consciousness at the center of my mind.

ENERGY
CONSCIOUSNESS

AURIC ENERGY FIELDS – YOURS AND OTHERS

ORIGIN: I understand that the source of all auric color energies originate in the first primal light energy of the Universe – the first Creator of unmanifest Spirit or God – the Christ Light or its equivalent in other spiritual traditions.

COLORS: I understand that every color has its own energy frequency.

THOUGHTS: I understand that certain color energy frequencies correspond to the nature of thought energies; positive, negative or variations of either.

FEELINGS: I understand that certain color energy frequencies correspond to feelings felt; positive, negative or variations of either.

INANIMATE OBJECTS: I understand that beyond the human aura, inanimate objects such as rocks, or anything that exists, may have its own auric field either originating from within it, or as a result of contact with outside energy fields. (Reference Psychometry.)

INTERACTIVE AWARENESS: I maintain an awareness in my life daily that my auric energy field can be interacting with the auric energy fields of people and objects exchanging positive or negative energies.

AURIC PROTECTION: Whenever I feel that I might be subject to taking in negative auric energies, I imagine or visualize a radiant white protective Christ or God Light all around my physical body.

PERSONAL: I understand that auric color energy, stimulated by the personal ego, is constantly in motion and changing.

SPIRITUAL: I understand that auric color energy frequencies of higher consciousness such as God, eternal love, wisdom, and mystical knowingness remain a constant in the auric field.

MEDITATION: I understand that my daily practice of meditation makes me more aware of what auras I am coming into contact with; positive, negative, or variations.

ACTIVATING SUCCESS ENERGY FREQUENCIES
IN YOUR MIND

DEFINING SUCCESS: I recognize that success, spiritually understood, means success of my life as a whole and is not limited to material or worldly definitions of success.

THOUGHT ENERGY: I understand that every thought I think is energy and that certain like energies exist in certain frequencies within my mind.

SUCCESS FREQUENCIES: I understand that there are various success frequencies, such as for financial success and success in love.

TUNING IN: I understand that success is achieved by consciously or unconsciously (karma), tuning into and being under the influence of success frequencies.

UNIVERSAL GOD MIND: I understand that all success frequencies exist and come from Universal Mind or God, which is at the innermost center of consciousness within me.

MEDITATION: Through my daily practice of meditation, I receive success frequencies into my conscious mind originating from the God Mind within me.

VISUALIZATION: Periodically during my daily activities, I visualize or imagine my body as filled with God's creating light energy, filling my conscious awareness with success energy frequencies.

SENSITIVITY ATTUNEMENT: Periodically during the day, to keep attuned to success energy frequencies, with one hand I touch the upper part of my body containing creative light energy success frequencies and with the forefinger of my other hand touch my forehead signifying that success frequencies are flowing into and influencing my conscious mind.

CLEARING THE MIND OF NEGATIVES – PART 1

CLEANSING MEMORIES: I recognize that I must cleanse my mind at all levels of negative thought energies that work against and come into conflict with positiveness that I both attempt to program into my mind, and from within, through the Universal Mind of God.

MEDITATION: I recognize that through my daily practice of meditation on God's Presence, at the center of my mind, that I draw into the memory levels of my consciousness sublimating light energy of God to change negative energy into positive light energy.

THOUGHT/FEELING MONITORING: The moment I think or feel negativity I immediately say to myself, "I nullify and neutralize that energy" before it can return to the memory level of my mind to continue to interfere with the establishment of positive God Consciousness.

VISUALIZATION: I daily take a few moments to visualize or imagine that the interior of my body is filled with positive universal God energy consciousness that sublimates all darkened negative energy into positive primal light or Christ/God energy.

CONSCIOUS REPROGRAMMING: Every time I have a negative thought or feeling, I immediately respond with an opposite positive thought which reprograms my mind with positive Christ Mind/Universal God consciousness energy.

EXAMPLES:

- Hate to forgiveness through Christ Mind/God's love.
- Anger to understanding the lack of Christ/God awareness in others.
- Jealousy to security in God realizing that jealousy is lack of God's Presence.
- Revenge to release, knowing that Karmic law is already in effect.
- Doubt to God centered identity in identity with universal power.

- Hurt to release to God's love, healing, and understanding of lack of others' awareness.
- Low self-esteem to oneness of identity with God's Presence within.

LIFESTYLE: I wear and surround myself with happy energy colors, listen only to beautiful, inspiring music, take time to enjoy the natural beauty of nature, and try to find the brighter, positive side of experiences that appear to be negative.

IDENTIFYING: I do not identify my identity with any temporary, negative experience, as I am not anything temporary, but am of the eternal positiveness and Christ light mind of universal God consciousness in which negative darkness ceases to be.

CLEARING THE MIND OF NEGATIVES – PART 2

AURIC PROTECTION: Every day I take a few moments to visualize or imagine an aura of white protective God light surrounding my body and shielding it from outside negative energy influences.

MUSIC: Whenever possible during my daily activities, I play beautiful music whose energy I feel myself absorbing into my body/mind energy field, transforming negative energies into positive energy.

HUMMING: When playing beautiful music, I hum to the music and feel that the humming energy vibrations are vibrating through my body/mind energy field, transforming negative energies into positive energy.

FRAGRANCE: I recognize that fragrance is energy, and so at least once daily, I expose my senses to a beautiful fragrance whose energies transform negative energies into positive energy in my body/mind/ spiritual energy field.

VOCABULARY: I choose to use words in my every day vocabulary that vibrate positive energy and avoid the opposite, knowing that negative word energy will enter my personal subconscious to adversely influence my conscious thinking.

CONVERSION ILLUMINATION: I affirm that in my daily physical body's processing, that negative thought and feeling energy stored in my subconscious memory is converted to waste matter and eliminated from my body as part of its natural functioning.

SUN ENERGY: Whenever the sun is shining, I take a few moments to close my eyes and imagine that positive sun ray consciousness energy is entering my body/mind energy field, transforming negative energies into positive energy.

CHRISTING: Daily, I take a few moments to visualize or imagine the positive energy body/mind field of Christ, seen as the figure of Jesus, entering into all parts of my body and that in such a positive God light energy field, negative body/mind energies are sublimated into positive, God light energy.

DEPROGRAMMING NEGATIVE ILLUSIONS

NEGATIVE ENERGY: I understand that negative energy is created through an illusion of personal selfhood or isolation or consciousness separation from the one life God, Creator of the Universe living in all created things, animate and supposedly inanimate.

NEGATIVE ENERGY ILLUSION: I understand that based on the illusion of personal selfhood, which includes, but is not limited to, fear, hate, vanity, greed, destructiveness, vengeance, limitation, victimhood, jealousy, envy, poor self-image, overly aggressive behavior, lust, and deceit.

MEDITATION: Through my daily practice of meditation, negative energy is sublimated into the light of Christ Mind energy consciousness.

VISUALIZATION: Daily, I take a few moments to visualize or imagine my body filled with positive God light where negative energy cannot exist.

SELF-IMAGE: I am filled with positive energy at all levels of my body, mind, and soul, declaring my oneness with God's spirit and my mind one with Christ/God consciousness.

AURIC PROTECTION: Daily, I mentally project a white protective aura of God light around my physical body as a protective shield against being influenced by outside negative thought/feeling energies.

NULLIFYING: Every time I think or feel a negative energy, I immediately nullify it so that it does not enter into or recede back into the personal subconscious memory level of my mind.

GOD POWER: I declare that the ultimate God power of the Universe exists in me to sublimate all negative thought/feeling energy into positive God light energy.

LIFE BEYOND THE PHYSICAL WORLD

CONSCIOUSNESS: I understand that all consciousness is part of the consciousness of the Universal Mind or God and that all that is – both physical life and the beyond – are contained within it.

SEEING: I understand that seeing that which is beyond physical sight perception is seeing into more of God's Consciousness within me.

ASTRAL DIMENSIONS: I understand that all dimensions of existence, including the physical, are varying energy frequencies of consciousness.

TUNING IN: I understand that the experiencing or seeing another dimension occurs when, in consciousness, I tune into the energy frequency of another dimension.

LOCATIONS: I understand that dimensions on varying frequencies of energy co-exist in the same location and are normally undetectable to each other except when paranormal perception takes place.

EXPERIENCE: I understand that life beyond the physical can be wide and varied together with the appearance of life forms, though most have the look of humans because those in the physical world are tuned into other worldly energy frequencies of a like nature.

HEAVENS: I understand that there are heavenly dimensions of consciousness corresponding to whatever religion, or lack thereof, a person believed in during their earthly physical life.

CONTACT: I understand that contact with other dimensions can come about through clairvoyant seeing into the other dimensions or astral body projection into another dimension.

MEDITATION: I understand that through my daily practice of mediation for the purpose of mystical union with God that I will experience various aspects of other dimensional existence as all is in the mind of God.

OVERCOMING OBSTACLES HOLDING YOU BACK

DEFINING OBSTACLES: In a greater reality of beingness, I understand that an obstacle is an energy obstruction in the environmental energy field which I function.

OUTGROWING: I understand that the most direct way to overcome an obstacle is to outgrow it by moving into a higher frequency of energy of consciousness.

CHANGE: I acknowledge in my own mind that to overcome obstacles, I must have a change in consciousness.

MEDITATION: Through my daily practice of meditation, I experience higher frequencies of energy, which lift me above the obstacle energy level closer to God's sublimating light.

VISUALIZATION: Whatever obstacle I wish removed, I visualize or imagine it in my mind being engulfed and sublimated by, and into, God's Light Presence to be no more.

RELEASE: Whatever accumulation of energy obstacles remain in my personal subconscious memory that I am no longer consciously aware of but are still energizing obstacles, I release for sublimation and healing into God's Light Presence within me.

NOT THE PERSONAL I - BUT GOD: I acknowledge that it is through God's Power Light Presence within me that obstacles are overcome in my life.

ALREADY SO: I acknowledge that in the mind of God at the innermost center of Christ Oneness, all obstacles that have been holding me back financially, in love, health, occupation, and creativity, are already overcome and in Universal Mind and Spirit; I am free to move forward and progress.

PRACTICING SPIRITUAL ENERGY SELF-HEALING

BODY ENERGY FIELD: I recognize that my body is an energy field of various energies.

ORIGINATING ENERGY: I recognize that all of the various energies in my body originate from one primal universal energy.

PRANIC/CHRIST/LIGHT/LIFE FORCE: I recognize that one primal universal energy is known by many names such as Christ, Prana, Light, Life Force, and is the source for all varying body energies.

CELL ENERGY: I understand that good health or ill health is dependent upon the energy activity in the cells of my body and that all cell energy is subject to the primal light of Universal Consciousness, or God, working through the Christ Mind.

AURIC ENERGY PROTECTION: Whenever I practice any spiritual energy self-healing, I project or imagine a white protection aura of God light surrounding my body with an energy shield from negative outside energies.

VISUALIZATION: When practicing, I imagine or visualize my body filled with primal light Christ Consciousness that enters into every cell of my body, adjusting the energy frequencies to maintaining good health or restoring it.

HOLISTIC: When practicing, I open all parts of my beingness; body, mind, and soul, to the healing light presence of universal Christ Mind/God Spirit.

MEDITATION: Through my daily practice of meditation, I connect with the primal light energy of universal Christ Mind/God Spirit presence to flow into every cell of my body; healing, adjusting, restoring, renewing, and bringing them into good health energy frequencies.

KARMA/TRAUMA: The all-powerful primal light energy of universal Christ Mind/God Spirit sublimates all negative karmic and trauma energies into perfect health frequencies of all levels of my mind and emotional being.

REINCARNATION - PAST AND FUTURE LIVES

AWAKENING: I understand that my earthly incarnations are in the twelve signs of the zodiac, that I experience each sign several times, and do so until I am once again in Christ awakened God consciousness.

PURPOSE: I understand that within our astrological natal birth chart is to be found the purpose of my soul for this life, including the positives and negatives of achieving it.

COLLECTIVE: I understand that I may be born as a part of a collective soul grouping, or group of souls, with a collective destiny of earthly experience.

OLD AND YOUNG SOULS: I understand that I may be part of a grouping of old or young souls, or spiritually awakened or spiritually unaware souls respectively.

TIME BETWEEN INCARNATIONS: I understand that young souls reincarnate more quickly due to their earthly attractions while old soul have a far greater period between incarnations, preferring a higher order of consciousness.

GENDER: I understand that a soul may incarnate as either male or female, according to the energy needs necessary for the awakening of the soul, or may incarnate as a gay person who is in a transitional state between genders energy wise.

KARMIC TIES/CONTRACTS: I understand that souls may incarnate and come together in the physical due to positive or negative karma, or to mutually agreed upon spiritual contracts of shared earthly experience.

ENERGY: I understand that based on the sum total of a soul's energy field that it is attracted to certain parents, geographical birth locations and the like, corresponding to the soul's energy.

HIGHER SOULS: I understand that souls automatically reincarnate until awakened to Christ/God consciousness, while those already awakened incarnate by choice to help unawakened souls.

SECRET POWER OF THE MIND

CONSCIOUS MIND: I recognize that my conscious mind is an outer energy emanating forth from innermost central consciousness or Universal Mind/Spirit God intelligence.

SOURCE: I recognize that the innermost central consciousness or Universal Mind/Spirit God intelligence is the ultimate source for all good that I can experience in this physical life and beyond.

WILL: I recognize that to have what is necessary to make my life what the Universe or God wants it to be that I must give up my personal will to the will of the creating presence of God within me.

CLEANSING: I recognize that I must cleanse the outer parts of my personal sense of mind of accumulated karma, trauma, and past negativity to open my conscious awareness to the Universal God Source within me to provide energized creating thought activity.

THOUGHT POWER: I recognize that creating thought power energy working in me is in proportion to what degree I have opened myself to my inner God Source and thus all creating thought energy is not of any personal selfhood, but of Universal God Presence working through me.

ONENESS: I recognize that the more I live in a consciousness of oneness with the Universal Source God Presence within me, the greater the creating power of thought energy within me to manifest good according to the will of the Universe which is God's Presence at the center of my mind's beingness.

MEDITATION: I recognize that through my daily practice of meditation I establish and maintain contact with my Universal God Source Energy to manifest God's purpose for my existence in this physical lifetime.

THE REAL SECRET: I recognize that the secret of my manifesting, creating, thought energy power is for the Universal God Thought Energy within me to think through me.

SEXUALITY IN SPIRITUALITY

ENERGY EXCHANGE: I understand that in all sexual activity there is an energy exchange that affects both people holistically affecting the physical body energies, mental energies at all mental levels, the spiritual level associated with the soul's purpose, and up to the God level depending upon how one with universal consciousness each participant is.

POSITIVE AND/OR NEGATIVE: I understand that energy exchange between people during intimacy can have a positive or negative effect on one or both people.

GRATIFICATIONAL OR RECREATIONAL SEXUALITY: I understand that sexual activity only for the sake of physical gratification of the body produces no lasting positive effect on the body, soul, or oneness with God, and leaves one empty in mind and soul with a void to fill, producing the need for more sexuality possibly leading to addiction.

KARMA: I understand that there may be karmic reasons for any sexual contact - individual, collective, or both - with the payback of negative energy or the reward of positive energy.

SOUL'S PURPOSE: I understand that the most positive sexual energy exchange is between two people in which the energy exchange helps one or both to better achieve their soul's purpose.

VERBAL SLANG: I understand that having a daily vocabulary expressing verbal slang of words of a sexual nature devalues sexuality and in turn the total consciousness of the individual is degraded, and the inner distance between the personal soul and the universal Spirit or God is greatly widened.

POSITIVE SEXUALITY: I understand that sexuality can have a positive energy effect on one's spirituality if there is love, friendship, or genuine caring between people that have initiated intimacy.

EXCITEMENT/STIMULATION: I understand that positive sexual energy exchange adding to people's spirituality is created more by inner connection than outer appearance, if the sexual attraction is to be lasting.

SPIRITUAL ENERGY HEALING

THE HUMAN BODY: I recognize that my body is an energy field comprised of many frequencies of energy.

THE HUMAN MIND: I recognize that the human mind is a field of energy – one with the energy field of my body.

PRIMAL LIGHT ENERGY: I recognize that primal light energy or Christ Mind Consciousness is the originating and controlling energy for both my body and mind's energy.

HEALTH CHAINS OF COMMAND: I recognize that the Christ Mind Consciousness in me controls the human level of my mind, and through this level, the energy consciousness frequencies throughout my physical body.

DRUGS: I understand that drugs reduced to their essentials are, in fact, energy frequencies that influence energy frequencies in the human body with an expectation of maintaining health as a preventative or restoring it.

MEDICAL TREATMENT: I understand that medical treatment through surgery, or any other treatment in the final analysis, is to change the energy frequencies throughout the body or in a localized part to bring about healing.

ALTERNATIVE MODALITIES: I understand that all alternative or complimentary healing modalities to traditional allopathic medicine are also, in fact, to change or maintain energy frequencies in tune with health.

MEDITATION: Through my daily practice of meditation, I am intuitively guided through the Christ Mind of my consciousness, one with God as to drugs, medical treatment, alternative treatment, and spiritual healing in regard to maintaining the health of my body, mind, and soul – or restoring it.

SPIRITUAL HEALING: I recognize that the absolute premise of spiritual healing is to establish healthful energy frequencies in my body, mind, and soul through the Christ Mind part of consciousness energy within me.

THE CHAKRAS - YOUR MIND AND GOD

CHAKRAS: I understand that there are seven primary energy centers of consciousness located in my body whose increased activation brings about spiritual awakening and perception of the nature of consciousness, God, and the Universe.

PART OF: I recognize that the chakras in my body are created and sustained by an individualized part of God's Consciousness within me.

ACTIVATION: I understand that further activation of the chakras coincides with an increased activity of the life force, or kundalini, and male and female energy consciousness within and encircling the spinal column on a higher than physical energy level.

ACTIVATING: I understand that activating the chakras into greater activity can be brought about through various meditation techniques, or can come about without techniques as a natural outgrowth of the soul's relationship to God's Presence.

THIRD EYE - INNER SIGHT - EYE OF THE SOUL: I understand that increased activation of my energy consciousness centers or chakras activates inner mind or higher consciousness perception, revealing spiritual mysteries beyond physical sight.

HIGHEST PERCEPTION: I recognize that the highest perception or goal of chakra activation is experiencing mystical union or oneness with God's Consciousness within me.

TOTAL ACTIVATION: I understand that total activation of all the chakras in my body in a single experience frees my individualized soul from the wheel of birth and rebirth, karma, and reincarnation.

GOD'S GUIDANCE: I release the activation of my chakra energy center within me to intuitively guide me and activate them according to the will of God for my soul's awakening.

UNSEEN MYSTERIES AFFECTING YOUR LIFE

ONE LIFE: I understand that ultimately there is but one mind in this Universe, manifesting as everything and everyone, including myself.

ONE MIND: I understand that ultimately there is but one life in this Universe, providing consciousness to what seems to be many minds.

MY EXISTENCE: I understand that ultimately, I exist as a thought form energy in the mind of God, inseparable from the mind of God.

THE UNIVERSE: I understand that the physical Universe is the physical manifestation of the mind of God in which I have my beingness on a physical level. "Within him we move, live, and have our being." Acts, 17:28.

ENERGY INTERACTION: I understand that the outer energy factors of my mind may be affected by environmental energies, and also by the ultimate primal inner energy, or God, through intuitive disclosure and guidance.

MEDITATION: I understand that through my daily practice of meditation, I more open the inner workings of consciousness within me so that my outer mind's energies are more affected by God's Presence containing guidance, healing, love, wisdom, and creativity.

TELEPATHIC INTERACTIONS: I understand there is contact interaction of energies between myself, others, and the psychic energy of my outer environment that can affect me positively or negatively.

AURA OF LIGHT: I understand that to safeguard myself from negative energy, I daily visualize a white protective aura of God's light surrounding my body from being negatively affectedly by others. "Put on your armor of light." Romans, 13:12.

DAILY DECLARATION: I am affected in all that I think, say, feel, and do by the light of God's Presence of the center of my mind, every moment of every day, consciously or unconsciously.

YOUR LIFE BEYOND YOUR FIVE SENSES

CONSCIOUSNESS: I understand that all consciousness is part of the consciousness of the Universal Mind or God and that all that is, both physical life and the beyond, are contained within it.

SEEING: I understand that seeing that which is beyond physical sight perceptions is seeing into more of God's Consciousness within me.

ASTRAL DIMENSIONS: I understand that all dimensions of existence, including the physical, are varying energy frequencies of consciousness.

TUNING IN: I understand that experiencing or seeing another dimension occurs when, in consciousness, I tune into the energy frequency of another dimension.

LOCATION: I understand that dimensions on varying frequencies of energy co-exist in the same location and are normally undetectable to each other, except when paranormal perception takes place.

EXPERIENCE: I understand that life beyond the physical can be wide and varied together with the appearance of life forms, though most have the look of humans, because those in the physical world are tuned into other world energy frequencies of a like nature.

HEAVENS: I understand that there are heavenly dimensions of consciousness corresponding to whatever religion, or lack thereof, a person believed in during their earthly physical life.

CONTACT: I understand that contact with other dimensions can come about through clairvoyant seeing into the other dimensions or astral body projection into another dimension.

MEDITATION: I understand that through my daily practice of meditation, for the purpose of mystical union with God, that I will experience various aspects of other dimensional existence, as all is in the mind of God.

HAPPINESS

ACHIEVING LASTING HAPPINESS

REALITY: I spiritually recognize that lasting happiness is not as a result of fortune, fame, power or anything limited by the transitory and temporary nature of human life or physical reality alone.

LASTING: I acknowledge that the only thing that is lasting is the eternal, and if I am to have lasting happiness, it must be associated and one with eternal happiness.

ETERNAL PRESENCE: I recognize that eternal presence is absolute reality existing everywhere, and I am a part of everything; it exists in me.

RECOGNITION: I recognize that to have lasting happiness I must contact and be one with eternal presence or absolute reality within myself.

MEDITATION: Through my daily practice of meditation, I open my body, mind, and soul to the energy beingness of eternal presence or absolute reality which my intuition interprets as God within myself.

REALIZATION: I realize that God, or eternal presence and absolute reality, is lasting happiness.

ONENESS: I recognize that to the degree that I am one with God's Presence within me, to the same measure do I experience lasting happiness.

CONTENTMENT: My lasting happiness is as a result of an ongoing awareness of my oneness with God's Presence within me which provides lasting contentment for my soul.

CREATING A GOOD KARMA FUTURE

CAUSE AND EFFECT: My thinking and actions of today are the cause that produces the effect I experience in my future.

BIBLE REFERENCE: As I sow (cause), so I reap (effect).

ONE ETERNAL MOMENT: In an absolute sense, there is but one eternal moment of time where both so-called present and future co-exist.

TIME: What I think and do now is instantly in effect as my future.

NULLIFYING: I nullify and neutralize all my negative thoughts and actions as they occur through the healing light power of God's Presence within me.

VISUALIZATION: I visualize or imagine God's Light Presence within me and see myself doing something good for one or more people.

PHYSICALLY: I am constantly on the alert as to some good I may do for someone as I go about my daily business in the physical world.

PAST NEGATIVE KARMIC INFLUENCE: Through the healing light power of God at the center of my mind, all levels of consciousness within me are healed of all past negative energy karma.

BENEFITTING OTHERS: In all that I think or do, I choose to think or do only such things as will in some way benefit one or more people.

MEDITATION: Through my daily practice of meditation, my consciousness is influenced by the goodness of God's Presence within me which cases me to think good things and do good things creating a good karmic future.

GOOD: I focus on experiencing good in my life to be in a better position to bring good into the lives of others.

ENDING YOUR YEAR POSITIVELY

ENDING/BEGINNING: I understand that ending this year positively establishes the energy that will start the New Year.

POSITIVENESS: I feel positive about the past year, as it has taught me many of life's lessons.

RELEASE: I release into the healing presence of God any and all negative energy feelings I may have experienced during the past year.

UNDERSTANDING: Through God's guidance received intuitively, I have a positive understanding of why things happened as they did.

FORGIVENESS: Through the power of God's Presence of love within me, I forgive everyone who I had bad feelings toward during the past year.

FAILURE: I regard any failure during the past year as a clearing in my mind of wrong goals so that God may guide me to success that I should experience according to God's Will for my life.

VISUALIZATION: I visualize or imagine the year just concluding and imagine that gray cloud-like negative energy is being sublimated into God's positive light energy, and that in its own way, the past year was a positive, successful one.

MEDITATION: Through my daily practice of meditation, the past year has been successfully positive, as through closeness to God, my year has been blessed.

GRATITUDE: I am grateful to God's Presence within me for having provided me with the power to overcome adversities while enjoying successful and positive times during the past year.

GETTING OUT OF YOUR OWN WAY IN LIFE

WHO IS IN THE WAY?: I acknowledge that there is a part of me that steps in front of another part of me when I attempt to do things.

PERSONAL SENSE OF SELF: I understand that the part of me that gets in the way is an illusionary sense of personal selfhood created by input from my external environmental experiences over a period of time.

PERSONAL SELF ATTRIBUTES: I understand that what gets in my way are one or more attributes of my outwardly conditioned personal self, which include, but are not limited to, the obstructive negative traits of fear, awkwardness, shyness, poor self-image, lack of self-esteem, past so-called failures, self-pity, victimhood, jealousy, hate, and guilt.

UNIVERSAL IDENTITY: I acknowledge that within me the real I of me exists in universal oneness with God's Presence at the center of my mind.

RELEASE: I release all darkened, negative thought energy traits of my illusionary personal self to the healing light of God's Presence within me to be sublimated and neutralized into light.

VISUALIZATION: I visualize or imagine that my personal illusionary self, like a gray shadow, disengages from my physical body, leaving my body filled with the light of God's Presence.

MEDITATION: Through my daily practice of meditation, I more completely establish and maintain a oneness or Christ-like state of identification with God's Presence within me, providing a clearer pathway to my goals, free of having an illusionary self get in my way.

TRAITS AND ATTRIBUTES OF MY UNIVERSAL GOD SELFHOOD: In oneness with God within me as my real Christed identity, I am one to pass through the illusions of personal selfhood via the power of God's attributes of eternal wisdom, will, creativity, healing, and love.

MAKING CHANGES...WHEN AND HOW

CHANGE: I recognize that making changes is a necessary part of life in order to improve and/or learn from human experience.

ETERNITY: I understand that I have a great sense of security by identifying with God's unchanging presence within myself, while living through necessary changes in my outer physical life.

MEDITATION: Through my daily practice of meditation, I am intuitively led and guided as to when and how to make changes in my life.

WHEN: I affirm and declare that I will intuitively know when to make changes, be it in my personal life, career, or any other area of my life.

COURAGE: I declare that I have courage to make changes, for I depend on God's Presence, wisdom, and power within me to provide what is necessary to make changes positively and effectively.

WILL: When making changes as with all else in my life, I give up my personal will to the universal will and power of God's Presence within me to accomplish necessary changes positively and effectively.

ALREADY SO: In God's mind within me, all changes in my life have already been accomplished at the right time and in a positive, successful way.

MY FUTURE: I affirm and declare that I am secure and at peace within myself that the timing and how to of all changes in my life are materialized into physical manifestation through God's Presence and power throughout my future.

OVERCOMING RESISTANCE TO POSITIVE CHANGE

RESISTANCE SOURCE: I realize that resistances to making positive changes in my life come from a personal sense of ego selfhood with its self-doubts about making even changes that would seem on the surface to improve my circumstances.

FEAR: I realize that personal ego mind fear may be a reason for resisting even positive change and so when I feel fear I turn immediately to my Christ Mind oneness with God to sublimate my fear into the light of God power courage within me.

UNKNOWN: I realize that I may resist positive change because of the unknown associated with the change and, instead turn inward to God's Presence that knows all that can be known, which thus removes a blockage of the unknown from my mind.

PUNISHMENT: I realize that God has already forgiven me for all that I believe I should be punished for and thus am free to make positive changes for my good at once.

RESPONSIBILITY: I realize that I may resist making positive changes because of doubting that I could handle the responsibilities, knowing that I will turn it over to God's Presence within me, which will surface to handle the responsibility.

POOR SELF-ESTEEM: I realize that resistance to positive change comes from poor self-esteem created by a personal ego mind sense of selfhood and thus choose, instead, Christ Mind awareness that my true self reality is always one with God and God's attributes.

NON-SUPPORT: I realize that resistance to making positive changes may come from feeling alone in my efforts or being non supported, thus I turn inward to God's Presence as my support in all I must do to improve my life.

POWERIZING HAPPINESS

REALITY: I spiritually recognize that lasting happiness is not as a result of fortune, fame, power, or anything limited by the transitory and temporary nature of human life or physical reality alone.

LASTING: I acknowledge that the only thing that is lasting is the eternal, and if I am to have lasting happiness, it must be associated and one with eternal happiness.

ETERNAL PRESENCE: I recognize that eternal presence is absolute reality existing everywhere, and as I am a part of everything; it exists in me.

MEDITATION: Through my daily practice of meditation, I open my body, mind, and soul to the energy beingness of eternal presence or absolute reality which my intuition interprets as God within myself.

REALIZATION: I realize that God, or Eternal Presence, and absolute reality is lasting happiness.

ONENESS: I recognize that to the degree that I am one with God's Presence within me, to the same measure do I experience lasting happiness.

CONTENTMENT: My lasting happiness is as a result of an ongoing awareness of my oneness with God's Presence within me, which provides lasting contentment for my soul.

SPIRITUALLY POWERIZING YOUR NEW YEAR

CLEARING: Through the healing and cleansing power of God's Presence within me, all levels of my mind containing negativity from the year just passed is cleared from my consciousness, totally and completely.

RELEASE: I release from my feelings, thoughts, and emotions all negativity towards one or more people, including jealousy, envy, hate, anger, and revenge through the all healing light presence of God within me.

SPIRITUALLY BASED POSITIVENESS: My thinking about the New Year is based on identifying my beingness with the positive attributes of God's Presence within me which is the foundation of my thinking positively.

SOURCE ACKNOWLEDGING: As I start a New Year and throughout it, I acknowledge that my source for all good in my life originates from God's Presence at the center of consciousness within me.

SEEK FIRST: As God is my source for all good in my life, my number one priority in the New Year is to seek out God's Presence within me, knowing that the more I increase my oneness, the more all things will be added to my life for good.

GOD'S WILL: I acknowledge that by doing God's Will I am actually doing the will of my highest self, one with God, through which my life is spiritually powerized in the New Year.

MEDITATION: Through my daily practice of meditation, I establish and maintain a closer oneness with God, which is my source for good in the New Year.

LIVING IN POWER: In my body, mind, and soul, I am powerized in the New Year by God's Presence flowing in and through me.

TURNING FAILURE INTO SUCCESS

BLESS AND RELEASE: I bless and release any so called failure of the past from all levels of my mind and simply regard it as a learning experience.

NOT THE EXPERIENCE: I recognize that I am not any failure experience, for failure experiences are only temporary and not part of my eternal self-oneness with God.

ELIMINATION: I regard all failure experiences to be part of an elimination process in the personal ego level of my mind to clear away all that is distracting me from what God's Presence wishes me to do to experience success.

ALREADY SO: I accept that in the mind of God at the center of consciousness within me that all seeming so-called failures of the past no longer exist and that only success for me exists in God's mind.

WILL: I give up my personal will, which may have past failure experiences associated with it, to the will of God, which contains my success within it.

GOD KNOWS: I accept that God knows my needs and creates success for me in accord for what is best for my eternal soul.

CONSCIOUSNESS: My mind is open daily to be filled with creative ideas that bring me success.

MEDITATION: Through my daily practice of meditation, negative failure energy is sublimated into God's light energy to bring forth creative success ideas into my awareness.

WHY YOU ARE A WINNER

TRUE SELF: I am a winner, for my true self is one with the presence of God at the center of consciousness within me, which makes me part of the Universal Mind/Spirit, the created, and all that exists.

SELF-IMAGE: I establish and maintain an image of myself as a winner due to and based upon my oneness with God.

ATTRIBUTES: In my inner oneness with God, I am a winner because I have God's attributes available to me to forever be a winner.

SO-CALLED FAILURE: Any so called failure is just one more experience of life to unmask and uncover the winner I have been right along.

MEDITATION: Through my daily practice of meditation, I establish and maintain a oneness with God, the eternal winner of all things individualized in me.

ALREADY SO: In the mind of God I am and have always been a winner, and in oneness will continue to be so through eternity.

ADAPTABILITY: In my oneness with God's Presence within me, I am adaptable to all the changes necessary to make in life that which makes and keeps me a winner.

CREATIVITY: The creative consciousness of God's Presence at the center of my mind flows through me to be a winner.

INTUITIVE GUIDANCE: I am a winner because my conscious mind continually receives intuitive guidance as to what to do to establish and maintain myself as a winner.

YOUR LIFE: LUCK, FATE, OR KARMA?

CAUSE AND EFFECT: I recognize that everything that takes place in physical life or beyond it is as a result of a cause which preceded effect.

LUCK: Based on the universal law of cause and effect, there is no such thing as luck or chance good fortune, as everything has a cause that precedes it.

KARMA: The law of karma best illustrates the law of cause and effect manifested in human experiences of good, bad, and degrees in between.

FATE: Fate covering a person's entire physical life, whether short or lengthy, can be as a result of cumulative karma of many lives or pre-physical existence.

DESTINY: Based on cause and effect, karma, and fate, each soul has a certain destiny to live in this or any other lifetime.

ONE ETERNAL MOMENT: Every soul is part of God's one eternal moment of time containing all they will experience over many lifetimes – bad, good, or in between.

CHOICE: I recognize that my soul has a choice as to what part of God's eternal moment to choose, and I choose enlightenment, which provides me with an awareness to choose good experiences.

MEDITATION: Through my daily practice of meditation, to one degree or another, I contact the presence of God's eternal moment and am energized by good experience energy.

ONENESS: In oneness with God's Presence, God provides me soul mastery to meet circumstances and conditions active in my life with positive, successful results.

Health
and
Well-Being

ACHIEVING INDEPENDENCE OF MIND AND SOUL

AURIC PROTECTION: Every day, I take a few moments to imagine and visualize a white protective light of God's Presence surrounding my body with protection from outer energy influences from the minds and souls of others.

MEDITATION: Through my daily practice of meditation, my conscious mind receives intuitive guidance from God's Presence to establish or maintain independence of my mind and soul.

PURPOSEFUL INDEPENDENCE: I recognize that my having real independence is being in tune with God's purpose for me in this lifetime, which keeps my mind and soul independent from the influence of others.

VIGILANCE: Every day, I retain a conscious vigilance not to lose the independence of my mind and soul by allowing others to influence or control me.

ONENESS: I recognize that the greater my oneness with God, the more inner power I have working within me to establish and/or maintain the independence of my mind and soul.

RELEASE: I recognize that to be truly independent in mind and soul, I release all mental and spiritual dependency on everything and everyone, and instead, manifest independence through my oneness with God's Presence within me.

KARMIC TIES: I release any and all karmic ties to others that my mind and soul may manifest my independence of God's spirit for me in this lifetime.

THINKING: I am an independent thinker influenced only by the wisdom thought process of oneness in God's Presence within me.

SOUL: I am an independent soul whose spirituality is controlled by the ultimate true life within me of God's Presence.

ELIMINATING SELF-DESTRUCTIVENESS

RECOGNITION: I recognize that the greatest obstacle to my success, health, and happiness in my life is the personal ego part of my mind from which self-destructiveness originates.

SUBCONSCIOUS INFLUENCE: I recognize that negative karma, trauma, and self-deflating experience stored as memories in my subconscious mind stimulates self-destructive thinking or actions and must be eliminated.

WHY?: I am divinely guided through the Christ part of my mind, one with God, as to specific subconscious, self-destructive, stimulating experiences that must be eliminated.

GUILT: I acknowledge at all levels of my mind that God forgives me for anytime I have erred, and that I don't have to destroy my life to make amends.

WORTHINESS: Through the power of the Christ part of my mind, one with God, I eliminate any and all sense of unworthiness from all levels of my mind that could be causing self-destructiveness.

FAMILY HISTORY: God's Presence within me, working through the Christ part of my mind, heals any family karma consciousness in all levels of my mind that could stimulate self-destructiveness.

VICTIMHOOD: Through the God power within me, working through my Christ Mind, I eliminate all sense of victimhood in all areas of my life and declare myself a God-created victor.

ESCAPISM: I find the answers I need in God's Presence and need not, therefore, escape into self-destructive escapisms, which only prolong my achieving success and happiness in life.

OTHERS: Through the God Presence within me I have the power not to succumb to being a part of self-destructive behavior of others whose paths cross mine.

NON-DEFEATIST: Through the Christ Mind God power within me, my attitude is at all times non-defeatist.

MEDITATION: Through my daily practice of meditation, whatever is necessary to my eliminating self-destructiveness surfaces to my conscious mind's awareness, while being internally healed by God's Presence within me.

HEALING A DIVIDED MIND

RECOGNITION: I recognize that to have power in my conscious spiritual thinking, that all stored up memories in my subconscious must be positive in nature.

CONFLICT: I understand that conflict between positive, spiritually-based thinking in my conscious mind will be compromised by conflicting negativity in my personal subconscious until my mind is healed and cleared of such content.

SUBLIMATION: I understand that I must spiritually sublimate all negative thought energies in my personal subconscious into a positive Christ Minded awareness into the light of God's Presence within me.

MEDITATION: Through my daily practice of meditation, I open the personal subconscious part of my mind to the healing light energy of Christ/God Presence that all negative trauma and karma be sublimated into light.

VISUALIZATION: Every day, I take a few moments to visualize that the entirety of my inner spiritual mind/body is filled with Christ/God light in which no negativity can live, and thus, my consciousness on all levels is healed.

BREATHING: Every time I exhale, I exhale negative thought energy out of me, and conversely, with every inhalation on a spiritual level, it stimulates the healing flow of Christ/God light into all levels of my mind.

CONSCIOUS THOUGHT CONTROL: Every time a negative thought surfaces from the memory level of my personal subconscious, I immediately affirm, nullify, and neutralize that thought so that it does not return to my subconscious.

ULTIMATE POWER: Through the ultimate power of Christ/God Light Presence constantly working within all levels of my mind, my mind is healed of all negative energies of trauma or karma from this or past lives.

HEALTH, GOD, AND YOU IN THE NEW YEAR

WITH GOD: With God's Presence working in and through my body, mind, and soul, my health in the New Year is cared for.

UNHEALTHY RELEASE: I release from all levels of consciousness throughout my body, mind, and soul, all self-images of myself as being an unhealthy person in this New Year.

HEALTHY SELF-IMAGE: Throughout my body, mind, and soul I have, and maintain, an image of myself in the mind of God that is that of a healthy person in this New Year.

MEDITATION: Through my daily practice of meditation, I open the consciousness of my body, mind, and soul to God's health maintaining and health restoring presence within me throughout the New Year.

VISUALIZATION: I visualize or imagine that God's Presence as light exists at all levels of my beingness; body, mind, and soul maintaining or restoring good health throughout the New Year.

MEDICAL: I am intuitively directed by God's Presence within me to the right doctors, treatment, and medications if I seek out medical means during the New Year.

SELF-STUDY: I make it a practice to study or be informed about health from allopathic medicine, alternative or complimentary healing modalities, and spiritual healing throughout the New Year.

PROTECTION: I give thanks to God's Presence within me for the protection in this New Year of my health in body, mind, and soul.

GUIDED: I am intuitively guided by God's Presence within me in everything having to do with maintaining or restoring good health in my body, mind, and soul throughout the New Year.

HOLISTICALLY RETAINING YOUTHFULNESS

HOLISTIC SELF-IMAGE: Daily, I maintain an image of myself as a total, holistic being comprised of a synthesis of body, mind, and Spirit, or God Presence.

ETERNAL IDENTIFICATION: I identify my spiritual beingness as one with the eternal part of me or the God Presence of consciousness within my mind.

ETERNAL YOUTHFULNESS: I recognize that the eternal part or God part of me is unchanging, and I identify with the idea energy of youthfulness contained within and as part of my eternal selfhood.

ETERNAL MOMENT: I recognize that ultimately all exists as one eternal moment of time, and that I choose to exist in the youthfulness part of the one eternal moment.

ATTITUDE: My daily attitude reflects my unchanging recognition of the youthfulness contained in the eternal God part of me.

MEDITATION: Through my daily practice of meditation, I establish and maintain 24/7 contact with the idea energy contained in God's eternal presence at the center of consciousness within me.

VISUALIZATION: I visualize or imagine God's eternal light presence containing the idea energy of youthfulness filling the interior of my body; first on a spiritual level, second on a mind level, and then into the center of every cell of my body on a physical level.

HUMOR: I recognize that humor has a positive effect on the health of my body, mind, and soul, and thus youthfulness, and God intuitively directs me to see the humor in many of life's experiences.

LOVE: I recognize that love is the greatest healing energy of all because it is the essence of God's nature, so I open myself to be a channel of love to others and in so doing this affects the health of my body, mind, and soul, which in turn helps me to maintain youthfulness.

CELL RENEWAL: Through the power of God's Presence within me, old cells are constantly being replaced with new cells throughout my body, helping me to retain youthfulness by affirming this renewing process daily.

INTUITIVE GUIDANCE: Through God's Presence at the center of my mind, I am intuitively guided as to what I should eat, what supplements to take, what exercise to engage in, and how to keep my mind energized with new learning, all adding to my retaining youthfulness.

ILLUSIONS AND REALITIES OF LIFE

APPEARANCES: My personal ego-intellectual mind may only be able to see the sensory illusion of something in the physical world while the Christ part of my consciousness, one with God's Presence within me, can see beyond any physical appearances to the reality of what really is.

GOOD AND BAD: What may appear bad to begin with may only be an illusion, blocking out the reality of good that will come about as a result.

SHORT AND LONG TERM: On a short-term basis, anything may give an illusion of good or bad, while the reality of whether it is ultimately good or bad can only be known on a long-term basis.

ONE LIFE: The physical life appearance illusion is that there are many lives on the planet, while the reality is that there is ultimately only one life; that of God in the entire Universe.

EXISTENCE: The illusion is that only this one lifetime exists for humans, while the reality is that everyone is inseparable from eternity, or God's Presence, and therefore, lives on eternally.

PERSONAL EGO-INTELLECTUAL IDENTITY: The illusion is that every human being seems to be a separate entity, while the reality is that only God's life exists hidden within, and manifests in the illusion of separate existences or humans.

LOVE OR ?: The illusion is that love might exist between two people, but the reality is that need and lust are posing as love unless the love of the one life of God flows between the two persons.

ALONENESS: The illusion is that you are alone unless you are with another person, while the reality is that you are always in the companionship of the only presence that really exits, God's life within and a part of you.

KARMA: The illusion is that one can escape the results of negative actions, or fail to reap the rewards of positive action, while the reality is that it's only a matter time when the karmic result materializes.

SPIRITUALITY: The illusion is that a person grows spiritually, while the reality is that they reawaken to what they already are on whatever level of spirituality that might be.

TRUE WEALTH: Wealth is not the illusion of what is contained in one's purse or wallet, but in warmth, joy, and love of the spiritual heart shared with God's Presence.

KARMA YOGA - A LABOR OF GOD

KARMA YOGA: I understand that karma yoga can lead me to achieving consciousness God union by achieving a union of my daily work with God's Presence within me.

MORNING DEDICATION: As I awaken and prepare for my work day, I dedicate the entirety of my work to God's Presence within me.

MIDDAY DEDICATION: At midday, I dedicate all that has happened in my work in the morning and all that will happen in the afternoon to God's Presence within me.

EVENING DEDICATION: At the conclusion of my work day, I dedicate all that has been a part of my work to God's Presence within me.

PRE-SLEEP DEDICATION: Just before going to sleep, I dedicate all my day to God's Presence, giving thanks for what I feel was good and releasing to God's healing presence all I feel was not.

MEDITATION: Through my daily practice of meditation, I attune my outer mind to God's Presence at the center of consciousness within me that God's Presence may be the true doer of my work.

INTUITION: Through my practice of meditation, God intuitively directs me throughout my work day and in all areas of my life.

WORK: Whatever work I do each and every day, it is God's Will that lives through my body, mind, and soul.

LIVING LIFE INTUITIVELY

RECOGNITION: I recognize that personal ego intellect is man-made and limited, while intuitive consciousness comes from God's Presence within me and is unlimited by its knowledge or reality and what should or should not be done in this life.

WORKINGS: I recognize that my personal ego intellect is a tool only to be used and directed through intuition by God's Presence within me.

MEDITATION: Through my daily practice of meditation, I open the conscious levels of my mind to receive intuitive guidance from God's Presence within me.

WILL: Daily, I release the will of my personal ego intellect to the will of God, which manifests as intuitive consciousness to direct me.

FIRST REACTION: I recognize that if I am meditating daily on God's Presence, while at the same time I have turned over my will to God's Will, that my first reaction to anything is God's guidance intuitively guiding me.

DECISION MAKING: In making decisions, I am more reliant on what I am sensing or feeling intuitively, than on something that I can analyze about it.

CREATIVE IDEAS: I recognize that the creative ideas that can dramatically change my life for the better come from God's Presence within me through intuitive consciousness.

CONTROL: All surface levels of my mind are controlled by intuitive consciousness, emanating forth from God's Presence within me.

MEDITATION TO MAINTAIN OR RESTORE HEALTH

MEDITATION: Every time I meditate, I open myself to the natural health maintaining and healing consciousness of God's Presence within me.

MEDITATIVE STATE: When I enter into what I know or believe to be a deeper state of meditation, I am ready to give my body, mind, and soul, healing thoughts.

HOLISTIC BENEFIT: Through my daily practice of meditation, God's Consciousness within me maintains good health or helps heal my total beingness of body, mind, and soul.

BODY: In meditation, the healing consciousness of God as primal Christ light energy maintains the energy factors and frequencies in my body for good health or heals the energies of my body as needed.

MIND: In meditation, all negative energies and trauma of the past are sublimated into the health maintaining and healing primal Christ light energy of God's Consciousness at all levels of my mind.

SOUL: In meditation, my soul's health is maintained or healed of negative past life energy or karma.

BALANCE: In meditation, the energies of my body, influenced by the primal Christ light of God's Consciousness within me, maintain or restore a balance, polarity, and harmony between my total body, mind, and soul beingness.

MYSTERIES OF BRIEF OR LONG LIFE

MEDITATION: I recognize that through my daily practice of meditation on God's Presence within me, eventually all mysteries of life are revealed to me.

PHYSICAL DNA: I recognize that physical DNA is the outer manifestation of spiritual factors.

SPIRITUAL FACTORS: I recognize that spiritual factors determining DNA, and in turn the length of a person's life include, but are not limited to, karma, lessons to be learned, and contributions of others.

CONTRIBUTIONS: I recognize that contributions to others include wisdom, healing, positive or negative role playing, and sacrificing.

LENGTH OF LIFE: I recognize that the length of a person's life, including my own, is when someone's soul's purpose for this lifetime has concluded.

OLD SOULS – BABY SOULS: I recognize that the length of a person's life is not determined by whether someone is an old soul or a baby soul.

GENERATIONAL: I recognize that the length of life may be influenced by incarnating as part of a soul energy grouping of souls.

MANNER OF EXIT: I recognize that nothing in this Universe is by chance, and that the manner of exiting this life is predetermined whether through natural, easy transition, long-term illness, accident, suicide, war, or tragedy.

TIME OF EXIT: I recognize that all in the Universe is controlled by God's inner presence and that the time when my soul or other souls depart is predetermined.

UNDERSTANDING: I recognize that the closer in oneness I am to God's Presence within me, the greater my awareness of the why behind the length of people's lives, inclusive of my own.

POWERIZING HEALTH

REALIZATION: In the New Year and throughout my life, the God part of me maintains my good health and heals me when healing is necessary.

INNER-OUTER COOPERATION: In this New Year and throughout my life, the inner part of my mind, one with God and the outer functional, environmental part of my mind, work in constant cooperation with each other to maintain good health or to heal me when necessary.

LISTENING: I am alert throughout my daily activities in the New Year to what my body is trying to tell me through various physical activities I feel taking place within it.

HOLISTIC RECOGNITION: In the New Year and beyond, I recognize that to maintain good health or to restore it, that health and healing is a whole process of having health in body, mind, and soul in an interactive way between these three major facets of my being.

NEGATIVITY RELEASE: I release from all energy factors of my body, mind, and soul all accumulated negativity prior to this New Year from my past to leave me with only positive spiritually powerizing energies for the present and future.

KARMIC RELEASE: In this New Year, I turn over my body, mind, and soul to the healing purification of God's light to sublimate into light all negative past karma that is or could adversely affect my health.

MEDITATION: Through my daily practice of meditation, I more thoroughly open to energies of my body, mind, and soul to the health maintaining, renewing, regenerating energies contained in God's healing light presence within me.

INTUITIVE GUIDANCE: Through my daily practice of meditation in the New Year and beyond, I am intuitively guided by God's Presence within me as to diet; supplements; alternative healing methods; healing practitioners; relaxation; recreation; physical, mental, and emotional conditions; and a life style conducive to maintaining good health or healing when it is necessary.

SPIRITUAL KEYS TO A QUALITY LONGER LIFE

CONSTANT RENEWAL: Through the grace of divine design by God's Presence within the consciousness of my physical body, I accept that new cells are constantly replacing old cells throughout it.

RELEASE: I release all negative thought energy of both the present and past so as not to have negative energy interfering with the positive energy of new cells throughout my body.

FORGIVENESS: I forgive everyone of everything in my entire life, knowing that old, negative energy adversely affects positive energy of new cells throughout my body.

MEDITATION: Through my daily practice of meditation, I bring forth the natural healing, restorative, reengineering energies of God's Presence within me into the new cells throughout my body.

SELF-IMAGE: I think and speak in a positive way about my age, such as referring to myself as so many years young rather than, so many years old.

MODERATION: I practice the great spiritual principle of moderation in all that I do including eating, drinking, exercising, and overall lifestyle.

MEANING: I am led by God's Presence within me to do something that gives my life meaning, such as being of service or help to others.

BRIGHT SIDE: The longer I live, the more I try to see the bright side of any situation or condition, knowing that God's bright light love presence is the eternal reality hidden, oftentimes, by the outer appearance of what seems to be contradictions to a bright side.

ENJOYMENT: Through God's Presence within me, I am led to have leisure activities that I enjoy with friends who can laugh, have fun, and be supportive of me, and I of them.

SPIRITUALLY MAINTAINING OR RESTORING HEALTH

BEINGNESS: I am a spiritual being created in God's light, and my physical body is an outward physical manifestation of my spiritual self-reality.

INTERPLAY: In matters of health, it begins with my soul, which in turn affects the individualized consciousness of my mind, and in turn, the consciousness of my body.

STARTING POINT: In reality, all matters of maintaining or restoring health begin with the spiritual health of my soul or my spiritual self-reality.

SOUL/SPIRITUAL SELF REALITY: I recognize the mystical reality that my soul is the individualized consciousness of God coming forth from the Christ light within me or that state of beingness where I and God exist in oneness.

MEDITATION: Through my daily practice of meditation, I establish and maintain Christ-like oneness with God in my soul, which in turn affects all levels of mind and body health wise.

VISUALIZATION: To maintain or restore heath, I visualize or imagine that my real body is that of God's Christ light – perfect, whole and complete – and that the light exists in every cell of my physical body, inwardly and outwardly.

MODERATION: I recognize that to maintain or restore good health, I must do everything in moderation, avoiding and finally eliminating excesses of all kinds.

BALANCE: I recognize that to maintain or restore good health, I must maintain a balance between my innermost spiritual beingness and outer mental/physical manifestation.

LISTENING: I am constantly alert to listening to what my body is trying to tell me in regards to any and all things pertaining to maintaining or restoring good health.

INTUITIVE GUIDANCE: In my ultimate state of oneness with God, I am intuitively led in regard to diet, exercise, rest, and all advice about my health from medical and all other claimed health experts.

GOD POWER: God power active in me has total power to maintain or restore good health throughout my soul, mind, and body.

TOTAL HEALTH

MEDITATION: Through my daily practice of meditation, I open my body, mind, and soul to the natural energies of God at the center of consciousness within me.

VISUALIZATION: Daily, I take a few moments to visualize or imagine my body filled with God's health-maintaining and healing light energy presence.

INTUITIVE GUIDANCE: Every day my conscious mind and feeling nature is open to receive intuitive guidance from God's Consciousness within me as needed for the health of my body, mind, and soul.

THOUGHT MONITORING: I monitor my daily thinking and feelings immediately saying, I nullify and neutralize all negativity affecting the health of my body, mind, and soul the very moment I think or feel anything negative.

CLEANSING BREATHING: With every inhalation, I breathe positive energy and with every exhalation, I breathe out negative energy to cleanse my body, mind, and soul.

EARTH AND SKY: Whenever I can, I take a few minutes to lie on the ground feeling God's healing energies of the earth beneath me while at the same time receiving the God healing energies of the sun overhead.

INTERACTION: My body, mind, and soul energies interact in harmony with each other and with God consciousness energy for maintaining or regaining my health.

HOLISTIC DIET: God consciousness intuitively guides me as to what I should place into my body, mind, and soul.

ONENESS: I declare that my first priority in life is my oneness with God, and through such oneness, God's perfection maintains health and healing throughout my body, mind, and soul.

ATTITUDE: I accept that in the health maintaining healing light presence of God, that God created me to experience health in my body, mind, and soul.

Love
and
Relationships

ATTRACTING AND MAINTAINING VALENTINE'S LOVE

KEY: I recognize that to attract and maintain valentine love, I must be one with those qualities that make one worthy of such love.

FRIENDSHIP: I recognize that to both attract and maintain valentine love, I must first be a true friend.

LIKING: I recognize that to both attract and maintain valentine love, both people must truly like each other, which is the basis of friendship and the foundation of maintaining love.

SUPPORTIVE: I recognize that to both attract and maintain valentine love, I must be naturally supportive and encouraging to the person I am with.

NON-JUDGMENTAL: I recognize that to both attract and maintain valentine love, I must be non-judgmental in expressing myself and seek God's intuitive guidance as to how to best communicate what I feel and think in a positive and constructive way.

NON-CONTROLLING: I recognize that to both attract and maintain valentine love, I must never attempt to control anyone, knowing that this is forcing a relationship to become or to continue to exist, which is contrary to all real love.

UNDERSTANDING: I recognize that to both attract and maintain valentine love, I should be understanding of the other person's views, lifestyle, why they think and feel as they do, and adjust through knowing accordingly.

TRUSTING: I recognize that to both attract and maintain valentine love, two people must be able to trust each other without reservation with details about their lives that they would not speak of to others.

COMFORT ZONE SHARING: I recognize that to both attract and maintain valentine love, both persons must feel relaxed and unguarded in sharing their thoughts, feelings, and time with each other.

ENERGY EXCHANGES BETWEEN YOU AND OTHERS

SOURCE: I understand that there is one primary light source or pure Christ energy from which all energies originate.

SELF: I understand that my body, mind, and soul are made up of varying energy frequencies that have originated from the primal Christ light source and are now individualized as a composite of myself in physical life manifestation.

PERSONALITY: I understand that the outer part of myself is the outermost manifestation of varying energy frequencies, both positive and negative, according to my karma and spiritual awakening or lack thereof.

INTERACTION: I understand that the energy frequencies that comprise my physical life selfhood can interact in energy exchanges with others in positive or negative ways.

SLOW/FAST: In simple terms, a slow energy frequency person may feel that a fast frequency energy person is too aggressive, reckless, or careless, while a fast energy person may feel that a slow frequency energy person is lazy, lacking initiative, not enthusiastic, or too slow of body or mind.

AURIC PROTECTION: Whenever I sense an energy disturbance between myself and another person, I immediately visualize or imagine a white protective Christ light around my body that cannot be penetrated by upsetting energy frequencies from another person or persons.

ENERGY ADJUSTMENT: Whenever I feel an energy frequency disharmony with another person, I immediately affirm to myself I am one with the allness of God's Presence within me, which raises me to a Christ energy level above all lesser energy and adjusts my energy frequencies to divine energy balance and equilibrium.

INCREASING LOVE IN THE NEW YEAR

RELEASE: I release from all levels of my mind any and all thoughts and feelings of lacking enough love in my life to the all healing light of God's Presence within me.

MEDITATION: Through my daily practice of meditation, I open all levels of my body, mind, and soul to God's Presence of ultimate love energy consciousness throughout this New Year.

AURIC EMANATION: I vibrate out the ultimate love energy of God, surrounding my body and attracting back love throughout the New Year.

TELEPATHICALLY: I am a sending station of God-powered, ultimate love energy being telepathically sent out 24/7 – attracting love back to me throughout the New Year.

LOVE MAGNET: Through God's ultimate love energy within me, I am a love magnet, attracting love to me throughout the New Year.

GIVER: I am a giver of love rather than a taker, and in so doing receive more love as love's essence, in and of itself, in giving.

LOVE'S EXPRESSIONS: Wherever I am, I am not limited to express only personal love, but find ways to express to people in general loving acts of kindness, caring, understanding, nurturing, forgiveness, compassion, and all other expressions that are Christ and God like.

GOD LOVES: I realize that the secret to having more love in my life during the New Year is to open my consciousness that God loves through my body, mind, and soul, using my physical manifestation as a vehicle or channel for divine love, which attracts love to me.

KARMIC RELATIONSHIPS IN YOUR LIFE

KARMA: I understand that karma means action and may be positive or negative, and that accumulated actions from this or past lives can influence my present.

KARMIC RELATIONSHIP: I understand that people who have been, are, or will be a part of my life may be drawn into a relationship with me, be it in love, family, parents, children, friends, co-workers, neighbors; anyone with whom I have a relationship.

COLLECTIVE TIME KARMA: I understand that I have a karmic relationship to those who are incarnating on earth at this time, be they my own generation, or generations before or after.

POSITIVE KARMA: I understand that good relationships are a result of good actions towards a person in this and/or past lives.

NEGATIVE KARMA: I understand that a negative or bad relationship is a result of negative or bad actions towards a person in this and/or past lives.

ENERGY EXCHANGE: I understand that all karmic relationships exist for the purpose of an energy exchange of consciousness between people to balance energy in both people involved.

OUTGROWING: I understand that a karmic relationship will continue between people until one or both outgrow the consciousness level of that which seems to keep them together.

SPIRITUAL PURPOSE: I understand that there always exists a positive spiritual purpose for the good of all parties concerned in a karmic relationship, even though this may not be outwardly observable at the moment.

LOVE??? IT'S MYSTICAL MYSTERIES

SOURCE: I understand that all things, including love, came from one original source or God.

ONENESS: I understand that all that exists, both seen and unseen, is a manifestation of God.

WHAT IS, IS: I understand that love is both symbolical and literal in its varying human manifestations.

KARMIC LOVE: I understand that people are brought together because of the existence or non-existence of love in their past.

LUST: I understand that lust is motivated by many factors inclusive of the need for love, which becomes manifest as physical gratification.

NEED: I understand that the need for love veils the real need for wholeness, completeness, or union with God.

ENERGY: I understand that the existence of love in its purest state of manifestation is primal light energy, first cause, or originating source.

SECURITY LOVE: I understand that love motivated by the need for security giving guises is the search for lasting security, the unchanging eternal, or God.

POSSESSIVE LOVE: I understand that the insecurity that motivates possessive love comes from not having found sufficient security of oneness with God's Presence.

CO-DEPENDENT LOVE: I understand that co-dependent love is motivated by an insufficient existence of oneness with God.

REALITY: I understand that there is one life, God, manifesting as everyone so that, in reality, all love is love of God or loving the God in another.

LOVING: I understand that all the varying human expressions of love are, in reality, God loving God.

MYSTICAL UNION: I understand that mystical union is the realization of the oneness, union of all, love, or God.

MOTHERHOOD VIEWED MYSTICALLY

MOTHERHOOD OF GOD: I understand that physical motherhood is an expression of the creative nature of God's spirit.

AS ABOVE, SO BELOW: I understand that the eternal and infinite creative process of God is made manifest in Motherhood.

GOD'S LOVE: I understand that God's love for the creations of Spirit finds a degree of expression in a mother's love.

THE GIVING OF LIFE: I understand that physical motherhood duplicates, in finite form, God's spirit of giving life throughout the Universe.

THE DIVINE FEMININE: I understand that even if a woman does not give birth, the divine feminine with all the qualities of motherhood lives within her and may be expressed in other ways.

INTUITION: I understand that intuition is part of the divine feminine in motherhood, or how God's Presence lovingly guides the surface mind or intellect.

MEDITATION: I recognize that my daily practice of meditation opens me to the influence of the divine creative motherhood energy of God to give birth to creative ideas and intuitive guidance.

MYSTICAL MYSTERIES BEHIND
LOVE RELATIONSHIPS

DESTINY: I understand that there are no coincidences in the Universe and that all love relationships have a karmic and/or spiritual reason to exist, be they momentary or a physical lifetime in duration.

REUNITING: I understand that through God's laws of karmic and spiritual cause and effect that I may be reunited in love before, during, or after this physical life with another person(s).

CONTRACTING: I understand that a pre-physical life contract or agreement may have been made with another person to share love in this lifetime.

ENERGY EXCHANGING: I understand that two people sharing love are in fact two energy fields exchanging energy consciousness with each other.

SEXUALITY: I understand that sexuality is a physical life symbol and energy culmination of mystical union with God in its lowest expression as lust and its purest expression when it is the culmination of love.

GOD WITH GOD: I mystically understand that love between two people is the God Presence within each person acknowledging, consciously or unconsciously, the God Presence in the other person.

MEDITATION: Through my daily practice of meditation, the fullness of God's love in me and the person I love is more completely and beautifully existent.

POWERIZING LOVE IN THE NEW YEAR

LOVE SOURCE: When I experience love, I recognize that the source of love is God's Presence within me, which is all things joined together in absolute unity.

GOD AS LOVE: I recognize God as love and love's presence within me.

EXPERIENCING LOVE: The closer my oneness to God's Presence as love within me, the greater my experience of love in my outer human self.

MEDITATION: Through my daily practice of meditation, I establish and maintain a closeness to a oneness with God's Presence as love within me, which manifests as a love energy in my outer physical life, attracting and maintaining love in my life in the New Year and beyond.

VISUALIZATION: Daily, I take a few moments to visualize or imagine that the interior of my body is filled with God's love as light and that light spreads to the outside of my body, forming an aura of love which attracts and maintains love in my life in the New Year.

LOVE'S POWER: I recognize the power of love as being the same as the power of God's Presence to positively affect health, healing motivation, and prospering in the New Year and beyond.

GIVING: I recognize that the more love I give, the greater the presence of love/God/energy, which attracts and maintains love in my life in the New Year and beyond.

LOVE MAGNET: I am a magnetic presence of love power, attracting and maintaining love through the power of God's love presence within me in the New Year and beyond.

CHANNELING: I am a channel for God's love in my daily life by giving the love of understanding, forgiveness, compassion, encouragement, and positive energy to others in the New Year and beyond.

PRACTICING SOUL-MATING

SOUL-MATES: I understand that soul-mates are just that, a mating of two souls.

COMMUNICATION: I understand that soul-mates are brought together on a soul-mate dimension, where communication over and beyond the physical exists.

ENERGY EXCHANGE: I understand that on soul-level dimension, communications are energy exchanges that transmit the equivalent of human thoughts and feelings, but at a higher spirited frequency level.

PHYSICAL SOUL-MATING: While I understand that soul-mate communication, for the most part, takes place on a soul dimension, that I can practice soul-mating in the world of my physical senses and dimensions.

MUTUAL MEDITATION: When meditating, I practice soul-mating by sitting together, preferably back-to-back, and letting the higher consciousness spiritual energy of our souls comingle and fuse.

HAND LIGHT EXCHANGE: I practice soul-mating by taking both their hands in mine and imaging the light of God's Presence within me flowing through my hands into theirs.

HEART-TO-HEARTH: I practice soul-mating by mentally visualizing or imagining that the light of God's Presence is flowing into my soul-mate's heart and theirs into mine.

MUSIC: I practice soul-mating with my soul-mate by allowing beautifully inspired music to take hold of both of us and sweep us upward in a musical simpatico of soul energy exchange.

SHARING: I practice soul-mating by sharing concerns, weaknesses, goals, and aspirations with complete trust, knowing that what is shared is a sacred trust because of the soul nature of the relationship.

SOUL-MATE RELATIONSHIPS

SOUL'S PURPOSE: I understand that a soul-mate's spiritual purpose in life must coincide with my own to be a true soul-mate.

SPIRITUAL: I understand that a true soul-mate is in harmony with my spiritual understanding of life.

SOCIAL/POLITICAL: I understand that a true soul-mate shares my social/political views.

LIFESTYLE: I understand that a true soul-mate is in accord and harmony with the lifestyle I choose to live.

HEALTH: I understand that a true soul-mate shares my views on health matters.

COMPLEMENTARY: I understand that a true soul-mate complements me, and I them, as a couple or combined energy field.

TRUST: I understand that a true soul-mate is someone I can trust, and they me.

RESPECT: I understand that a true soul-mate is someone who I respect, and they me.

FORGIVING: I understand that a true soul-mate is someone who is quick to forgive me, and I, them, for whenever either of us has erred.

SUPPORTIVE: I understand that a true soul-mate is supportive of my efforts in life, and I of theirs.

COMFORTING: I understand that a true soul-mate is there to comfort me in time of genuine need, and I of them.

CONFIDANT: I understand that a true soul-mate is someone I can confide in without hesitating, knowing that I would not be betrayed in the future, and they have the same faith in me.

THANKFUL: I understand that a true soul-mate is someone that I am continually thankful for, and that they have the same feeling toward me.

TELEPATHIC LOVE ENERGY IN YOUR LIFE

THOUGHT ENERGY: I understand that every thought I think is energy.

FEELING ENERGY: I understand that every emotion I feel is energy.

LOVE: I understand that all thoughts and feelings of love are energy.

PRIMAL ENERGY: I understand that there is one energy from which all other energies are created.

UNIVERSAL MIND: I understand that primal energy is the first creation of God or Christ light energy.

TELEPATHIC MEDIUM: I understand that all energy moves within the primal light energy from one creation to another, whether human, animate, or inanimate.

TELEPATHY: Whatever love energy I think or feel travels through the medium of primal Christ light energy.

24/7: I understand that whether I am awake or asleep, my love energy thoughts and feelings are being broadcast out telepathically.

TELEPATHIC LOVE RECEPTION: I understand that love energy thoughts and feelings may be received consciously or unconsciously by all of humanity, as well as specific people, and may be accepted or rejected according to the karma or God's Will active in them in this lifetime.

MEDITATION: Through my daily practice of meditation I establish and maintain a greater oneness with the ultimate, absolute God love energy.

GOD LOVE ENERGY: The more God love energy is active in me, the more I telepathically send it out to others, which attracts and maintains more love in my life.

TELEPATHY BETWEEN YOU AND OTHERS

MYSTICALLY VIEWED: I understand that there is but one mind in the Universe that is God's mind, and that all that takes place does so in the mind of God, inclusive of telepathy between people.

BIBLE REFERENCES: I understand that the words in the Bible – within him, we move, live, and have our being – refers to the God Mind and all activity therein inclusive of telepathy between people.

BEGINNING: I understand that all thought, inclusive of telepathy, is transferred from the unconscious mind of one person to the unconscious mind of another person, some of which may become conscious, or if not, still influence the conscious thought activity of the receiver.

MEDITATION: I understand that the daily practice of meditation opens the conscious level of my mind to unconscious thought activity, and thus, telepathic sensitivity to another person's thoughts.

EMOTIONAL TELEPATHY: I understand that emotional telepathy, or charged thought energy, can travel between people, such as love or opposite extremes of ill feelings.

SLEEP: I understand that what I am thinking or feeling, consciously or unconsciously, can travel between me and another person, though I am asleep, as this is an unconscious activity.

PROTECTION: Anytime that I may sense any negative thought or feeling coming at me from another person telepathically, I project a white protective aura of God light all around my body.

TELEPATHY WITH GOD: I understand that telepathy between my conscious mind and God's mind at the center of consciousness within me, comes to me as intuition as thought, feeling, or both.

TO HAVE LOVE, BE LOVE

SOURCE: I recognize that God's Presence is the absolute presence and source of love.

ONENESS: I realize that the greater my oneness with God's Presence of love within me, the more I am one with the absolute presence of love itself.

I AM: The more I am one with God's love, the more I am love itself.

MANIFESTING: The more I am God's love itself, the more I manifest the attributes and qualities of God's love.

ALL LEVELS: I communicate all levels or expressions of love, be it friendship love, family love, co-worker love, neighborly love, or personal love.

MEDIATION: Through my daily practice of meditation, I connect in thought and feeling with the presence of God's love or personal love.

AURA: I visualize or imagine my body surrounded with an aura or pure white God love energy, which I give out to others with whom I have contact.

TELEPATHY: On an unconscious level of my mind, I am constantly telepathically sending forth God's love energy to those I know, and the world in general.

COMPASSION: As love, I am compassionate towards others and extend compassion to them.

FORGIVENESS: As love, I am forgiving of others for their lack of awareness and weaknesses.

UNDERSTANDING: As love, I am understanding of people, their needs, their strengths and weaknesses, and why they are as they are.

ENCOURAGEMENT: As love, I communicate encouragement to others who need support in their lives.

I AM: As love, I am the living, breathing, communicating presence of God's absolute love expressed daily.

BEING: By being love expressed, I have and live in an abundance of love in my life.

UNCONDITIONAL PERSONAL LOVE

NEEDS: It is natural for me to always be placing the needs of the person I love before my own.

EXPECTATIONS: I do not create expectations in my mind as to what I expect of the other person and from the other person and, therefore, am not disappointed or angered.

FORGIVENESS: I unconditionally love and, therefore, I unconditionally forgive.

CONTROL: There is no need to attempt to control the person I love, for my unconditional love loves them in spite of anything that they might do that I would try to control.

MONEY: My relationship is not based on whether there is or is not money, because my love is unconditional for them.

HEALTH: In sickness as in health, my love remains constant, for it is unconditional.

LIFESTYLE: Through mutual divine guidance from God's Presence, we live a lifestyle where we can express unconditional love to each other in the way we live our lives.

INTIMACY: Whether physically expressed on not, due to health or age, unconditional love begins and culminates more in the exchange between our souls than our bodies.

MEDITATION: Through my daily practice of meditation, I contact God's unconditional love presence within myself, which I share as unconditional personal love.

YOUR LOVE KARMA – EXPLORING IT – PART 1

GOD AS LOVE'S PRESENCE: I realize that I could not have love in my life or even know of its existence unless God, whose presence within me, is the source of love.

GOD IS LOVE: How close I am to God is how loving I am.

GOD KNOWS: I realize that before I even ask about love in my life, that God's Presence within me knows exactly what I most need in love and provides me with such experience.

LEARNING: I realize that the experience of love in my life eventually teaches me about the nature and reality of love, or the nature and reality of God.

AS YOU GIVE: I understand that as I give God's love through me to others, they give love back to me to the degree that they are capable of love.

PAST KARMA: I recognize that good or bad karma in love can be as a result of good or bad actions from previous lives, as well as my present one.

CHRIST MINDED LOVE: I recognize that being in oneness with God or Christ Minded, I have more and better love in my life by being understanding, compassionate, forgiving, and supporting of others.

MEDITATION: Through my daily practice of mediation, I open my mind, body, and soul to God's love presence, which in turn attracts and/or maintains love in my life.

YOUR LOVE KARMA – EXPLORING IT – PART 2

PAY OFF KARMA: I understand that two people are brought together as a result of bad past deeds in love by one or both persons.

REWARDS KARMA: I understand that a harmonious love relationship exists when two people are brought together as a result of good past actions in love by both persons.

ENERGY BALANCING KARMA: I understand that two people may be brought together in love to achieve a balance within each of thought, emotional, and spiritual energies.

LEARNING EXCHANGE KARMA: I understand that two people may be karmically drawn to each other in love to mutually share experiences to better learn the various aspects of life.

REBOUND LOVE KARMA: I understand that rebound love karma draws two people together to ease the hurts of one or both persons.

SHORT TERM LOVE KARMA: I understand that short-term relationships act as a love energy filler to learn from until meaningful love is experienced.

NEEDY LOVE KARMA: I understand that needy love is an illusionary love, which is an attempt to get from another person what seems lacking in oneself or one's life.

SYMBOL LOVE KARMA: I understand that symbol love is formed by one or both person's attraction to money, worldly power, notoriety, intellectualism, position, accomplishments, or spirituality that is seen as what each person symbolizes to the other.

WHOLE PERSON LOVE KARMA: I understand that whole-person karma takes place karmically when two people, who are whole within themselves, form a synthesis of body, mind, and soul.

SPIRITUAL LOVE KARMA: I understand that spiritual love karma brings people together to share the learning and energy presence of the love of God within each.

MYSTICISM

ACTIVATING GOD POWER WITHIN

WILL: I step aside daily (my personal will) and allow God's Will to be totally in charge of my life.

SURRENDER: I totally surrender my body, mind, and soul to be used by God's Presence.

CHRIST MIND: In the Christ Mind part of my consciousness, awareness of my oneness with God exists as the ultimate real life of my body, mind, and soul.

DOER: I recognize and declare that God is the doer in all that is done, every day of my life.

CREDITING: As God is the real doer, I credit God alone for all good that takes place in my life, be it in love, health, material needs – whatever my real needs according to God's Will for my life.

MEDITATION: I practice meditation daily, knowing that it activates bringing the presence, and thus the power, of God into my conscious mind and daily life.

GOD KNOWS: God already knows what is best for me, be it in love, health, material needs, and all else, and I totally accept that it is already so in the mind of God.

ALREADY SO: I declare that God's Power has already been active in my life - today and for all my tomorrows that have already been lived in God's single moment of eternity, alpha and omega, the beginning and end as one.

ASCENDING LEVELS OF SPIRITUALITY

MANY LEVELS: I understand that there are many levels of spirituality from the most primitive and basic of the baby soul level to the most advanced old soul, Christ-like level, and that each level affects a person's human life in some way.

NATURE WORSHIP WITHOUT CHRIST AWARENESS: I understand that at the most basic level that human beings worship nature objects without an awareness of a Supreme Creator.

GOD'S, GODDESSES, ANGELS, SPIRIT GUIDES: I understand that humans can ascend from nature worship to physically experience dimensions of gods, goddesses, angels, and Spirit guides, or a psychic tourist trap for baby souls.

GOD - OUT THERE: I understand that human awareness may ascend from god/goddess/guides, and angel dimensions to an awareness that there is a Supreme Creator out there, in the form one would imagine God to be in.

TRADITIONAL ORTHODOX: I understand that from an awareness of a Supreme God/Creator that my soul may live in an in-between zone where spirituality is organized religion and there is a need to belong to a group.

NEW AGE: I understand that many people, having outgrown religious dogma, will look to finding a different lifestyle in New Age approaches, such as psychism, psychic readings, tarot, and crystals; all of which tend to remove the central focus from God centeredness to objects or the return to other dimensional entities.

METAPHYSICAL: I understand that a metaphysical approach to spirituality may encompass a combination of psychological and philosophical approach to age old questions of life's mysteries, such as "Who am I? What am I?" and similar questions of the mind and spirit.

MYSTICAL: I understand that the final ascension of spirituality of an old soul occurs at a mystical level or direct experience of an inner state of onement consciousness with God.

HUMAN LIFE EFFECT: I realize that every level effect that a person may be on affects their daily life in matters of health, material needs, love, and other matters of human concern.

ASTROLOGY, MYSTICISM AND YOU

DIVINE DESIGN: I understand that the solar planetary alignment of nature at any given point of time and space is by divine design of Universal Consciousness or God.

AS ABOVE - SO BELOW: I understand that the outer design of solar planetary positions is mirrored as focal points of energy in my inner unconscious mind.

NATAL MAP: I understand that my natal or birth chart is a spiritual map of my unconscious with which I can work.

KARMA: I understand that my natal chart reflects the karma I have entered this life with, to work with God to eliminate karmic weaknesses and debt and above all, to use the full potential of the positive karma with which I have incarnated.

12 ZODIAC SIGNS: I understand that my soul incarnates into all twelve zodiac signs many times, each time eliminating more of the weakness while strengthening the positives of each sign.

WHEEL OF BIRTH AND REBIRTH: I understand that upon mastering the attributes of all twelve signs and/or reaching mystical union with God that I break the wheel of birth and rebirth and no longer have to incarnate into this physical realm except by choice to do so.

MEDITATION: I understand that through the practice of daily meditation with my focus on God's Presence, I will eventually achieve mystical union, which will free me from the zodiacal wheel of birth and rebirth.

SPIRITUAL GUIDE MAP: I understand that my natal chart can be likened to a spiritual guide map for my life by using the full potentials for good and positiveness, while at the same time working to sublimate the negatives into light - and in so doing, living the will of God in my life.

MEMORIES OF THE PAST AND OF THE FUTURE

PAST MEMORIES: In my heart I honor the memory of those I have loved and those dear to me who have passed on or are no longer a part of my physical life, yet remain an eternal part of God's Presence within me with which I am one.

TIME AND SPACE: In fond memories of those close to me at some time in my life, I declare that neither the illusion of time and space separates them from me in the consciousness of God within me.

LOVE: To special people who are part of memories past and memories to be lived in the future, I send you my love.

MEMORIAL DAYS: On memorial days, I especially take time to go back over the years to thank those who have meant so much to me in my life.

WAR: For those who I have not known but who have sacrificed a portion of their body, mind, or entire physical life for me, I honor in gratitude eternally.

REALIZATION: I realize that whatever life I am currently living will be part of my future memories, and thus, I am especially motivated to express my love, friendship, affection, and gratitude to those close to me in the present, who will be part of my memories in the future.

ETERNITY: Whatever has been or will be lives in one eternal moment of God's Presence in oneness with my soul.

FUTURE MEMORIES: I honor God's Presence for my divine origin in whom memories of past, present, and future co-exist as one eternal moment.

MYSTERY OF TIME - A KEY FOR MASTERING LIFE

TIME: I recognize that what appears to be the passing of time is, in truth, one eternal moment.

ONE MOMENT: Eternity as an absolute reality is one eternal moment of time, containing the appearance of past, present, and future.

GOD'S PRESENCE: God's Presence lives in absolute time or one eternal moment of past, present, and future.

CLOSENESS: The closer I am to God's Presence within me, the closer I am to one eternal moment of time which is God's mind in manifestation.

NOW: Living in the eternal moment of now, I live in the energy consciousness of the future and all that can be.

EXISTENCE: All that could ever be mine already exists in the eternal moment of time.

ONENESS: In inner oneness with God, I am one with the eternal moment where past, present, and future are one.

THE FUTURE: In oneness with God's Presence within me as one eternal moment, the future is now.

ALREADY MINE: All that I or my life can be is already mine and exists in one eternal moment of God's Presence.

KEY: Through my daily practice of meditation, I experience future good in love, health, material needs, and all else by recognizing the eternal now and by releasing my personal will to it which is God.

THE PRESENCE: To the degree I am one with God's Presence, I am one with the eternal now, and I am all that can be.

ETERNITY: I am the presence of eternity or God individualized into human form.

PARTNERING WITH GOD

REALIZATION: I realize that there ultimately is but one life in the Universe as there is in my body, mind, and soul, and that life is God.

VEHICLE: I recognize that my body, mind, and soul are vehicles through which God's spirit, mind, will, and purpose may be expressed.

RECOGNITION: I recognize that I am an individuation of God's mind/spirit individualized into human form.

CHOICE: I choose to enter into a partnership between the manifestation of my body, mind, and soul, and the will, mind, and spirit of Almighty God.

WILL: I turn over all awareness of my personal will to the will of God that it be done through my body, mind, and soul.

COOPERATION: The outer human manifestation of consciousness within me opens itself to fully cooperate with the innermost consciousness of God.

PACT: I agree to a cooperative pact between the personal and universal, the soul and spirit, the outer and inner mind, living and manifesting in and through me at all levels of my beingness.

MEDITATION: Through my daily practice of meditation, I open my body, mind, and soul to universal God energy consciousness to manifest through me.

INTUITION: I am guided in cooperative partnership with God through intuitive guidance that God's Will for my existence be fulfilled.

PRACTICING MYSTICAL ONENESS
WITH GOD DAILY

MEDITATION: Through my daily practice of meditation, my surface level mind is either in conscious or unconscious contact with Universal Consciousness or God in an inner state of oneness.

VISUALIZATION: Every day, I take a few moments to visualize or imagine that the entirety of the interior of my body is filled with God's Light Presence, and I am one with that presence.

AWAKENING: Daily upon awakening from sleep, I affirm and declare that I live this day in mystical oneness with God.

RETIRING: Daily, when I am ready to retire to sleep, I affirm and declare that during sleep I am in mystical oneness with God.

DURING SLEEP: During sleep daily, my mind is influenced by my oneness with God for guidance and thoughts are planted in my subconscious for coming forth into my surface mind level.

RELEASE: Daily, I affirm and declare that I choose to live my life in oneness with God and God's Will for my life and so release my personal ego self to live my universal selfhood united with God.

AT MEALS: Daily, at every meal I take time in my own mind or in some other way to acknowledge that the food before me is made possible by my oneness with God.

ACCOMPLISHING: Daily, all that I do or accomplish is as a result of my oneness with God to whom I give credit as having been the true doer for all achieved.

LOVE AND BLESSINGS: Daily, I take a few moments in my awareness of my eternal oneness with God to send forth into the atmosphere the love and blessing of God's Presence to everyone, everywhere.

PRECOGNITION - GLIMPSING THE FUTURE

THE ETERNAL NOW: I understand that time and space in spiritual reality exist in one eternal moment of time.

COEXISTING TIME: I understand that in spiritual reality the past, present, and so-called future coexist simultaneously.

ILLUSION: I understand that in spiritual reality, time is an illusion of the physical senses due to the need for dualism to give created life validity.

PAST LIFE RECALL: I understand that since many people have had past life recalls or glimpses of one or more previous lives, the past continues to live or have reality in consciousness.

FUTURE LIFE GLIMPSES: I understand that since people, such as Nostradamus, or Bible references, such as Revelations, have claimed to have glimpsed the future and that this could not be done unless the future already exists.

HOW: I understand that glimpses of the future may take place during a dream; in a half waking or meditative state of mind, or during a non-analytical relaxation of the personal ego thought process.

MEDITATION: I understand that my daily practice of meditation increases the possibility of opening to future consciousness connected with my own life or anything in the future in general.

CAUTION: I understand that I should be cautious of anyone claiming to see the future at will as future glimpses are spontaneous in nature and blocked by the exertion of the personal will.

SENSING AND KNOWINGNESS: I understand that glimpses into the future can be visual. They can also be a sensing or knowing of the more immediate future based on the instinctive survival mechanism in the collective unconscious of humanity.

PSYCHIC SIGHT . . . SEEING BEYOND

CHRISTIAN REFERENCE: I understand that reference to psychic sight, the third eye, or seeing beyond within, exists in the New Testament in the words, "If thine eye be single, thy body shall be filled with light."

END GOAL: I understand that the end goal of paranormal sight is mystical union or union with God.

MEDITATION: I understand that I may have paranormal visionary or psychic sight perceptions as I move progressively toward mystical union.

DIVERSIONARY: I understand that while some paranormal sight experiences have a fascination connected to them, I will not become diverted by them from my end goal or mystical union with God.

SIGHT STAGES: I understand that paranormal sight perception generally starts in the forehead area, then the entire inner head area, next to the interior of the body to the reproductive area, and finally, in mystical union where there is no sense or physical body, only infinite God Light Presence.

EXPERIENCES: I understand that paranormal sight experience may vary greatly, some of which may include vibrant colors, energy patterns, vortexes, symbols, gods or goddess images, architecture, and religious symbols of various degrees.

EYES OPEN OR CLOSED: I understand that most paranormal sight perception is seen inwardly, but may also be seen with physical eyes open if mind contact has been made.

I-THOU: I understand that in paranormal psychic sight perception that I retain my sense of individuality from what I am perceiving, or an I-Thou relationship.

MYSTICAL UNION: I understand that in mystical union with God, all sense of I-Thou is non-existent, and there is only oneness with God's light.

PSYCHISM AND MYSTICISM EXPLAINED

SIMILARITIES: I understand that similarities between the physical and mystical may include paranormal sight and extra-sensory experience.

PERSONAL: I understand that psychism deals with the personal or mortal aspects of consciousness.

IMPERSONAL: I understand that mysticism involves that which transcends personal ego consciousness, the impersonal or universal consciousness.

PSYCHISM: I recognize that the experiences of psychism may include, but are not be limited to, other dimensions, clairvoyance, clairaudience, visions of symbols, scenes, gods, goddesses, or any other paranormal experience involving an I-Thou relationship.

MYSTICISM: I understand that the practice of mysticism is for the sole purpose of first hand, direct experience of the absolute, eternal/infinite beingness as Mind/Spirit Consciousness – God.

MEDITATION (PHYSICAL): I understand that mediation, even for that sole purpose of union with God, may be filled with experiences of a psychical nature.

PSYCHICAL LEARNING AND DISTRACTIONS: I understand that while I may learn of life's mysteries from psychical experiences, that they are distractions that can direct my attention away from my ultimate spiritual goal, or union with God.

STATE OF BEING: I understand that while psychical experiences may be revealing or interesting in and of themselves, they may keep me just as neurotic or incomplete, or even more so if I allow myself to get caught up in such experiences and miss becoming a whole person, or union with God.

MEDITATION (MYSTICAL): I understand that the number one priority of my daily meditations is to transcend my personal ego consciousness to experience universal beingness or union with God.

RESULTS FROM PRAYER – THE HOW AND WHY

PRAYER DEFINED: I understand that prayer in the Christ Mind part of my consciousness is in truth really the practice of mediation.

ENTRANCE: Whenever I pray (meditate), I enter into my own mind (closet) and shut the door behind me (close off outer senses), and pray (commune in consciousness) with my Father (God) which seeth in secret (in the higher consciousness within me). Matthew, 6:6.

GOD WHO KNOWS: I recognize that the presence of God in my mind already knows what I truly need. Matthew, 6:8.

RESULTS: I understand that what is asked in prayer is only answered if it is Christ Mind Consciousness mediation in which God has inspired the prayer. Matthew, 21:22.

GOD INSPIRED PRAYER: Through living in prayerful (meditation oneness) with God, it is God who creates or inspires the prayer which is to bring the conscious human part of my mind into alignment with God's Will to manifest through me.

CHRIST MIND PRAYER: I recognize that in Christ Mind Consciousness, it is God who places a prayer into my mind to be prayed.

ALREADY SO: I understand that all Christ Mind prayer is under the influence of God and is successful because it is already so in the mind of God.

ALIGNMENT: I recognize that Christ Mind prayer is an alignment of the moral part of my mind with what is already so in the immortal Christ/God Mind.

INTUITIVELY CREATED PRAYER: God intuitively gives me knowing of what to prayer for based on what is best for me, and it manifests as it is already so in the mind of God.

SEEING THE BEYOND WITHIN

SEEING: I recognize that my mind has the capacity to see into itself and study itself as consciousness.

LEVELS: I realize that my mind exists on many different levels that my mind can see into.

HEAVEN: I understand that certain levels of consciousness that are significantly spiritual in nature can be inwardly seen.

VARIETY: I understand that the mind looking into itself can visually see a wide variety of perceptions.

THIRD EYE SIGHT: I understand that the interior region of my forehead is open to view realities existing beyond physical life experiences.

FULL BODY SIGHT: I understand that my conscious mind's awareness is open to inner visual experiences in the interior of my upper body down to the reproductive area.

ENERGY: I understand that energy normally used by the outer five senses is turned inward to active inner sense perception.

MEDITATION: Through my daily practice of meditation, I open the surface level of my mind to receive inner sense visual perceptions.

AURA: Whenever I practice meditation, I visualize a white, protective aura of God's Light, emanating from within me and surrounding my physical body with light.

GOAL: My foremost and primary goal is to perceive God's Light Presence or ultimate oneness where I, the viewer and the viewed, and God are one.

SPIRITUAL ESP IN YOUR LIFE

SPIRITUAL ESP: I understand that spiritual ESP is centered on the intuitive interaction between my conscious mind, Christ Mind, and Universal Mind/Spirit Consciousness, or God.

MEDITATION: Through my daily practice of meditation, I establish and maintain spiritual ESP in the interacting of all levels of consciousness within me, from the surface level to the innermost mind/spirit God level.

VISUALIZATION: I visualize or imagine that the entire interior of my body is filled with Christ/God Light, flowing into my conscious mind or spiritual ESP.

INTUITION: I open my conscious awareness to intuitive guidance from the Christ/God center of Universal Mind/Spirit within me.

THOUGHT GUIDANCE: Intuitive ESP thought energy flows into my conscious awareness, daily guiding me in love, health, material needs, and all else necessary according to God's Will in my life.

FEELING GUIDANCE: Intuitive ESP feeling energy flows throughout my body's conscious energy field, producing in me guidance feelings in love, health, material needs, and all else necessary according to God's Will for my life.

WILL: To clear my consciousness of obstacles to intuitive spiritual ESP, I give up my personal will to God's Will for my life.

STILLNESS: Periodically during the day, I become still in body and mind that I may sense intuitive ESP guidance from God's mind/Spirit within me.

THE GREATER YOU

THE LESSER OR FALSE YOU: I recognize that the lesser or false me is that which is not eternal and subject to temporary and fleeting states of selfhood and cycles of life with corresponding limitations.

THE GREATER ME: I recognize and accept that there is a changeless and eternal part of me that is the Christ Mind of my mind's beingness, or that which is one with God and thus the greater me.

ONENESS: I recognize that the greater Christ part of me - one with God - is capable through oneness to manifest the greater me in my life.

RELEASE: Daily, I release any and all sense of lesser, limited, false selfhood to the light of God's Presence within me that it be sublimated into the greater Christ/God beingness with which I am one.

WILL: Daily I open myself to God's Will within me that is, in truth, the will of my greater Christ selfhood.

MEDITATION: Through my daily practice of meditation, my greater Christ Mind self is energized in body, mind, and soul.

VISUALIZATION: I daily take a few moments to visualize or imagine that the interior of my body is filled with God's Christ light body of my greater self.

MATERIAL NEEDS: My greater Christ Mind self - one with God - who knows my material needs before I ask, supplies me with all that I truly need for the good of my soul and therefore my body and mind.

LOVE: I affirm that my greater self is one with God's Presence of love and therefore attracts love into my human life.

HEALTH: I realize that my greater Christ Mind is always aware of the greatest perfection of health with which the greater Christ part of myself is one.

Happiness: The greater me exists in an ever on-going state of happiness because of my Christ Mind oneness with the eternal God part of me.

YOUR FUTURE – CO-CREATING IT WITH GOD

WILL: Throughout my body, mind, and soul, I choose to do the will of God's Presence within me today, which creates what my future will be.

MEDITATION: Through my daily practice of meditation, I open the surface levels of my mind to the thought/feeling energy of God's Presence to influence my future.

INTUITION: Through my daily practice of meditation, God's Will is intuitively made known to my conscious thought/feeling nature to guide me in creating a better future.

NEEDS: God's Presence in me knows exactly what I most need to create a better future and intuitively guides me to create it.

GOD-CHANNELING: God's Will, my needs, and God's needs for creating me are one in the same and therefore my outer mortal manifestation is a channel for God's Presence.

CO-CREATING: As God's Presence within me is in charge of my mortal manifestation, my mortal manifestation co-creates my future with God's wisdom, healing, love, and blessings.

ABOUT THE AUTHOR

As far back as he could remember, Paul Leon Masters was drawn to the mysteries of life, the Universe, the human mind and soul, and the presence of a Higher Intelligence behind creation.

Dr. Masters spent countless hours with thousands of people conducting higher consciousness research, all of which enormously expanded what he originally learned in the 1950s and early 1960s. He founded the National Metaphysics Institute in 1965, conducting research on the spiritual heights and potentials of mind and spirit, which produced even more information from which he could teach.

Dr. Masters' contributions to the field of mystical psychology were those of a trail-blazer. Having founded the University of Metaphysics (1976), he then founded the International Metaphysical Ministry (1989) to accommodate the worldwide interest and enrollment in his courses. Fourteen years after that, he founded the University of Sedona (2003). He deservedly earned recognition as the world's foremost teacher of metaphysical doctors, teachers, and ministers, offering self-paced, distance-learning degree programs in Holistic, New Thought, Theocentric, Transcendent, and Transpersonal Metaphysics.

Both universities have a curriculum that is strictly non-secular and theological in nature, and they have become the world's largest schools of their kind, spanning 120 countries.

The education that Dr. Masters has provided since 1959 has produced an international alumni and student population that reaches out to transform the world. The evolving curriculum, based on decades of consciousness research, offers timeless teachings that connect people to their real soul, inner-self, God Presence.

https://universityofmetaphysics.com
https://universityofsedona.com
https://internationalmetaphysicalministry.com
https://metaphysics.com
https://voiceofmeditation.com

SPIRITUAL RESOURCES

Mystical Insights - Knowing the Unknown

Dr. Masters' dedicated over five decades of full-time, professional work involving the research and application of his findings to improve human lives. His soul's fulfillment was to share how universal mystical presence and psychic/mystical energy factors influence every aspect of our lives. Dr. Masters explores these concepts and shares his realizations and wisdom with *Mystical Insights*. Available from Amazon.com.

Daily "Improve Your Life" Audio Message

The Daily "Improve Your Life" Audio Message is a spiritual, metaphysical 3-5 minute discourse offering enlightening inspiration and upliftment.
http://universityofmetaphysics.com/category/daily-improve-your-life-audio-message/

Inspirational Lectures

Listen to inspirational lectures that Dr. Masters presented between 2006 and 2008. Almost all of these videos began with a meditation or healing treatment, after which he presented a teaching and sometimes included an affirmation and a closing meditation.
https://metaphysics.com/paul-leon-lectures/

Weekly Mystical Insights

The Weekly Mystical Insights are a composite, or synthesis, of what is described as the transcendent, the transpersonal, the psychical, and the mystical, or Universal Consciousness, or God.
https://universityofmetaphysics.com/category/mystical-insights/

Timeless Wisdom Series

Since 1959, Dr. Masters conducted research and teaching into the exploration of consciousness, synthesizing results from research experience with science, psychology and the mystical teachings of Christ and others.

https://metaphysics.com/timeless-wisdom/

Voice of Meditation

When listening to these recordings, vibrational frequency energies within Dr. Masters are transferred through his voice into the conscious and unconscious levels of the listener.

https://voiceofmeditation.com/

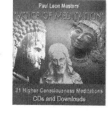

***

If after reading *Spiritual Mind Power Affirmations* you feel compelled to take your studies further, we welcome you to join our ever-expanding, international student body. Please visit our website: www.universityofmetaphysics.com.

For further information, please call:
In USA: 1-888-866-4685
International: 1-928-203-0730
or email uom@metaphysics.com

https://universityofmetaphysics.com
https://universityofsedona.com
https://internationalmetaphysicalministry.com
https://metaphysics.com
https://voiceofmeditation.com

90038919R00085

Made in the USA
Columbia, SC
25 February 2018